1 PETER:
LIFE AS AN OUTSIDER

Robert H. Thune

STUDY GUIDE WITH LEADER'S NOTES

New
Growth
Press

newgrowthpress.com

New Growth Press, Greensboro, NC 27401
newgrowthpress.com
Copyright © 2022 by Robert H. Thune

Cover Design: Faceout Books, faceoutstudio.com
Interior Design and Typesetting: Gretchen Logterman
Exercises and Application Questions: Jack Klumpenhower

ISBN: 978-1-64507-242-3 (Print)
ISBN: 978-1-64507-243-0 (eBook)

Printed in the United States of America

29 28 27 26 25 24 23 22   1 2 3 4 5

CONTENTS

INTRODUCTION

Displaced. That's what it feels like to be a Christian in an increasingly post-Christian world. You fit in, but not entirely. You're welcome in some places, but not in others. You speak the language and understand the culture, yet you don't quite feel at home.

You're far from the first to feel this way. Christians throughout history have struggled with the tension of living in two worlds. On the one hand, we're citizens of God's kingdom, defined most deeply by our allegiance to Jesus and to his gospel. On the other hand, we're residents of some particular city and state and country, living at a specific time in history. The question in every age is how these two citizenships fit together—or how they don't. How much of our culture can we embrace? What should we reject? How can we live respectfully among neighbors who don't share our convictions, while still holding firmly and faithfully to biblical truth?

That's why we need to study 1 Peter. Peter wrote this letter to Christians scattered throughout the Roman Empire in the late first century. They, like us, were wondering how to live gospel-shaped lives in the midst of a contrary culture that ostracized them. Their *questions* were not exactly the same as ours, but their *challenges* were. New Testament scholar Karen Jobes writes, "Slander and malicious talk undermined their relationships with associates and family, threatened their honor in the community, and possibly jeopardized their livelihood. The issues of how to maintain a vital Christian faith in such circumstances and how to respond to such unjust treatment pressed upon them."[1]

Peter's epistle is a book uniquely suited for our cultural moment. During the two decades I've served in pastoral ministry, dramatic shifts have taken place in the cultural landscape of North America, where I live—as they may have where you live too. People have become more strident in their political views, more suspicious of Christianity, and less open to religious conversation. Social media and smartphones have come to dominate our lives, replacing face-to-face interaction with mediated, digital connection. Every topic—from sexuality to ecology to education—has become politicized. Christian unity is crumbling; tribalism and fragmentation abound. In a moment like this, what does faithful Christian discipleship look like? How can we joyfully thrive as God's people in the face of opposition and uncertainty? That's the question we need to answer, and it's where Peter's first epistle can help us.

So let's dive in together and learn from this amazing book of the Bible. Along the way, I hope you'll find your presuppositions challenged, your thinking stretched, and your affections stirred.

HOW TO USE THIS STUDY

Like the other books in this series, this study guide will help you study the Bible with a focus on Jesus—like Peter has in his epistle. This book is designed for a small group setting. Peter wrote to believers who were their own community within a larger culture. His encouragement and guidance are meant to be practiced *in community*, where believers can repent and learn kindness and trust Jesus and work through hardships *together*. With this in mind, try to make the group a place where participants can be open about the struggles and sufferings of life. Not everyone will be equally quick to share personal concerns—and that's okay—but these lessons will create opportunities for that to happen.

Each participant should have one of these study guides in order to join in reading and be able to work through the exercises during that part of the lesson. The study leader should read through both the lesson and the leader's notes in the back of this book before each lesson begins. Other than that, no preparation or homework is required.

There are ten lessons in this study guide. Each lesson will take about an hour to complete, perhaps a bit more if your group is large. It will include these elements:

BIG IDEA. This is a summary of the main point of the lesson.

BIBLE CONVERSATION. You will read a passage from 1 Peter and discuss it. As the heading suggests, the Bible conversation questions are intended to spark a conversation rather than generate correct answers. The leader's notes at the back of this book provide some insights, but don't just turn there for the "right answer." At times you may want to see what the notes say, but always try to answer for yourself first by thinking about the Bible passage.

ARTICLE. This is the main teaching section of the lesson, written by this study guide's author.

DISCUSSION. The discussion questions following the article will help you apply the teaching to your life.

EXERCISE. The exercise is a section you will complete on your own during group time. You can write in the book if that helps you. You will then share some of what you learned with the group. If the group is large, it may help to split up to share the results of the exercise and to pray, so that everyone has a better opportunity to participate.

WRAP-UP AND PRAYER. Prayer is a critical part of the lesson because your spiritual growth will happen through God's work in you, not by your self-effort. You will be asking him to do that good work.

Peter's epistle will invite you to examine both the hardships of life and the hope you have in Jesus. Where these meet is where the Spirit often does his work, shaping you to be more like your Savior. Pray for that to happen as you study this part of God's Word together.

1

ELECT EXILES

BIG IDEA

We who believe in Jesus are both elected by God—bound to him in a covenant sealed by blood—and exiles in the world.

BIBLE CONVERSATION *20 MINUTES*

The book of 1 Peter was written by the apostle to believers in parts of modern-day Turkey, a mostly non-Jewish region of the Roman Empire where several churches were founded in the decades after Jesus ascended to heaven. The book's opening lines include references to the history of God's people:

- The **Dispersion** means God's people living outside the promised land and among foreign cultures.

- **Exile** was the event following the Babylonian conquest of Jerusalem, about 600 years earlier, that first forced many of the people to live abroad.

- **Sprinkling with blood** evokes the covenant God originally made with his people centuries earlier, when he gave them his law at Mount Sinai and they first became his holy nation.

For more context, read about the covenant ceremony as described in Exodus:

> Moses wrote down all the words of the Lord. He rose early in the morning and built an altar at the foot of the mountain, and twelve pillars, according to the twelve tribes of Israel. And he sent young men of the people of Israel, who offered burnt offerings and sacrificed peace offerings of oxen to the Lord. And Moses took half of the blood and put it in basins, and half of the blood he threw against the altar. Then he took the Book of the Covenant and read it in the hearing of the people. And they said, "All that the Lord has spoken we will do, and we will be obedient." And Moses took the blood and threw it on the people and said, "Behold the blood of the covenant that the Lord has made with you in accordance with all these words."
>
> Then Moses and Aaron, Nadab, and Abihu, and seventy of the elders of Israel went up, and they saw the God of Israel. There was under his feet as it were a pavement of sapphire stone, like the very heaven for clearness. And he did not lay his hand on the chief men of the people of Israel; they beheld God, and ate and drank. (Exodus 24:4–11)

With that background in mind, have someone read **1 Peter 1:1–2** aloud. Then discuss the questions below:

Christian believers were rare at that time in the Roman Empire. How would living then as a believer in Jesus be similar to life as a Jewish exile, and how is similar to your life today?

How might Peter's description of believers in verse 2 encourage you when you feel like an exile?

What features of the covenant ceremony at Mount Sinai help you appreciate what it means to be sprinkled by Jesus's blood—to be a person for whom he died? Explain.

* * * *

Now read this lesson's article, written by the study guide's author. Take turns reading it aloud, switching readers at each paragraph break. When you finish, discuss the questions that follow the article.

Lesson

ARTICLE

WHO WE ARE

5 MINUTES

As I begin to write this article, I'm sitting in my front yard on a pleasant summer evening, looking up at the trees planted by the master gardener who previously lived at this address. The majestic red oak in the middle of the yard stands tall and stately. The aspens rustle in the breeze. And the spruce along the sidewalk puts forth fresh needles in a brighter green than the darker, older ones that persisted through the winter.

Each tree's identity determines its behavior. The evergreens don't put out leaves, the oak doesn't bear pinecones, and the aspens don't drop needles. What each tree *does* is grounded in what each tree *is*. Even Jesus observed, "Figs are not gathered from thornbushes, nor are grapes picked from a bramble bush" (Luke 6:44).

What's true in nature is also true among human beings. Our behavior flows out of our identity. *Who we are* determines *how we live.*

So, as the apostle Peter begins this crucial letter to God's people scattered throughout the Roman Empire, he reminds them of who they are: "elect exiles." Like the original readers, we too are elect exiles. And understanding *who we are* will shape our behavior.

ELECT

In individualistic, equitable Western societies, we frown upon the idea of anyone choosing something *for* us. We like to make our own choices and control our own destinies. The idea that we are God's elect—chosen and set apart by him—can sound to modern ears like we are puppets on strings, pulled about by a capricious deity.

But that's not the vision Scripture gives us. To the biblical writers, the doctrine of election is not controversial or contentious in the least, nor does it erase our decision-making. Each of us must come to Christ personally, embracing him in faith and trust. But above and behind our decisions stands God's choosing of us. In the same way God chose Abraham and Isaac and Jacob to be his covenant servants, so he chooses each Christian believer.

And this election is a Trinitarian accomplishment, involving Father, Spirit, and Son. God's people are chosen "according to the foreknowledge of God the Father, in the sanctification of the Spirit, for obedience to Jesus Christ and sprinkling with his blood" (v. 2).

The historic Christian creeds and confessions generally move from Father to Son to Spirit. But Peter's order is Father-Spirit-Son. Why? Perhaps because that's how we actually experience the work of the Trinity in salvation. The Father has chosen us to belong to him, but he makes his election come to pass in time and space and history by the work of the Holy Spirit. One biblical scholar speaks of God "taking hold of a person from the inside." That's a great way of describing what happens in us when the Holy Spirit awakens us to our need for a Savior.

And when the Holy Spirit does that work in someone, he doesn't bring them into some sort of generic spirituality. He brings them into God's new covenant founded on Jesus Christ and on his crucifixion. That's why the text references "sprinkling with his blood." Peter is drawing a connection to the covenant ceremony described in Exodus. In the ancient Near East, when two parties would enter into solemn relationship with one another, they would sacrifice an animal. The blood of that animal would seal the covenant. It was a symbolic way of saying: if one of us breaks this covenant, may we be killed as this animal.

In the same way, God has established a covenantal bond with his people through the death and resurrection of the Lord Jesus Christ. We belong to him, and he belongs to us. Our covenantal relationship with Jesus makes us take obedience seriously, producing in us a heart-cry that says, "All that the Lord has spoken we will do!" At the same time, Jesus's blood is God's sacred vow that when we do sin, he will take away the guilt and shame of our covenant breaking. He will set us apart and train us to live in the honor and joy of obeying him, and one day he will bring us into his kingdom to worship around his throne and feast with him at his table. "Grace and peace," as Peter says, are ours in abundance because of God's great love.

EXILES

Exile is a dominant theme in the Old Testament. After generations of idolatry and rebellion, God cast his people out of the promised land. Scattered among the pagan nations, God's people hoped to return to their homeland one day.

Peter refers to the Christians living in Asia Minor as "the Dispersion," a term used in the first century to refer to the Jewish population living outside Jerusalem. By referring to Christians in this way, he's reminding us that we too are living outside our homeland. We are exiles, strangers, foreigners. Our citizenship is in heaven.* Because we belong to Jesus, we are never fully at home in this world.

Grasping our identity as exiles helps us understand how to live within a pagan society. Rather than *withdrawal from* the world or *assimilation to* the world, we can practice *faithful presence within* the world. Exiles don't withdraw from the society around them, but neither do they forget their homeland and their distinct identity. As New Testament scholar Karen Jobes puts it: "Foreigners dwell respectfully in their host nation but participate in its culture only to the extent that its values and customs coincide with their own that they wish to preserve."[2] That's the Christian way of living in society. Respectful, but different. Present, but distinct.

CONCLUSION

To live life joyfully and courageously as outsiders, we must have a well-grounded sense of identity. We who belong to Jesus are elect exiles. We have a distinct relationship with God, and a distinct relationship to the world.

An easy way to remember this is to visualize the cross. The vertical beam reminds us of our relationship to God (elect). The horizontal beam reminds us of our relationship to the world (exiles). This isn't the core meaning of the cross, of course, but it's a good way to keep in mind who we are as people saved through the cross. It's a helpful reminder of the identity-shaping truths that stand right here at the beginning of 1 Peter. So, Christian: never forget who you are.

---

* Philippians 3:20

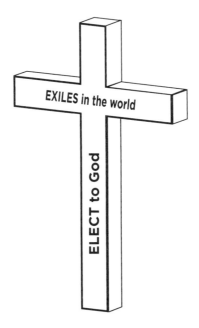

DISCUSSION *5 MINUTES*

How does the label *elect exile* compare with other words you have used to describe yourself as a Christian? What's helpful about the *elect exile* description?

If you more often remembered that you are bound to Jesus in a covenant sealed by blood, how might you live differently?

EXERCISE

LIFE AS AN EXILE
20 MINUTES

Life as an exile is not easy. For this exercise, you'll work on your own to think about how you handle being an exile in the world. Work by yourself to respond to both parts of the exercise, writing in the book or making notes if you find that helpful. At the end of the exercise, you'll share and discuss some of your responses with the group.

NOTE: This exercise, like many others in this study guide, assumes you consider yourself a believer in Jesus. If you are not a believer yet, or are unsure, using 1 Peter to study the life of a believer can still be a great help to you. Simply adjust the exercises to fit your situation: tell what you find attractive or troubling about the Christian life, or how you face some of the same struggles a believer might, etc.

PART 1: Tell something about your life as an EXILE in the world. For each item below, pick the statement that is most true of you and then briefly explain it. (Both statements might be partly true, but pick one that fits you best.)

Do you WITHDRAW or ASSIMILATE?

☐ I am more likely to <u>withdraw</u> from the world, isolating myself from my neighbors and from non-Christian elements of society. This dulls my witness to others because I have little contact with them or act as if we have few shared experiences.

☐ I am more likely to <u>assimilate</u> into the world, forgetting that I'm a citizen of God's kingdom and loving the things of this world as if they already offered all I need for happiness. This kills my witness to others because I have nothing distinct or better to offer them.

Briefly explain: What is one way you often withdraw or assimilate?

Do you feel a need for COURAGE or COMFORT?

☐ I have recently experienced active opposition to living for Jesus. I have a growing awareness that my life as an exile in this world will involve suffering and will require <u>courage</u>.

☐ I have recently felt disheartened by how the world rejects Jesus. I have a growing awareness that I need the <u>comfort</u> of Christ as I live in this world.

Briefly explain: How have you suffered because of your Christian life, or what has discouraged you?

Have you left behind SIN or WORLDLY HONORS?

❐ I am especially aware of <u>sin</u> I have repented of (or am still struggling against) as I determine to obey Jesus in this world filled with temptations.

❐ I am especially aware of <u>pleasures, comforts, or honors in this world</u> that I have foregone or missed out on because I am treasuring God's kingdom instead.

Briefly explain: What have you given up for Jesus, knowing he is worth it?

PART 2: Although you are still an exile *in the world*, your greater exile and estrangement from God is already ended if you believe in Jesus. You are God's ELECT. Choose a few truths from the list below that might especially encourage you as you deal with the struggles you noted above. Be prepared to explain why you find those truths helpful.

❐ I remember that my heavenly Father knows me by name and has personally chosen me to glorify and enjoy him forever.

❐ I know that the Spirit will continue to tug at me from the inside, drawing me away from sin and to God, which gives me confidence that I can indeed grow in holiness.

❐ I remember that I am included in God's family, with all its privileges. I am loved, protected, provided for, listened to, disciplined for my good, and given an everlasting inheritance kept in heaven for me.

❑ I know that I belong to Jesus in a covenantal bond, bearing his name and participating in the glory of sharing in his sufferings. This surpasses all worldly honors.

❑ I can be sure that, by Jesus's blood shed for me, I am forgiven of all my sin.

❑ I remember that, by Jesus's blood shed for me, I am also released from my bondage to sin and selfishness. I am now able to live for him, set free to be the godly person he created me to be.

❑ Other: _____
_____.

When the group is ready, share some of your responses. What has your life as an exile been like?

What truths about who you are as God's elect might help you in your struggles as an exile? Explain why those truths are helpful.

WRAP-UP AND PRAYER *10 MINUTES*

Prayer is a way we turn to God for help rather than trying to grow by our own strength. Pray together about the items you discussed in the exercise. Ask your Father to help you know who you are in Christ, and to give you courage to live as exiles in the world.

2

A LIVING HOPE

BIG IDEA

The resurrection of Jesus gives us grace upon grace: a living hope anchored in the past, sustaining us in the present, and pointing us to future glory.

BIBLE CONVERSATION *20 MINUTES*

Having reminded us *who we are* in Christ, Peter begins the main message of his letter with praise for *what we have* in Christ. This is summarized by the phrase *living hope*. Have someone read **1 Peter 1:3–12** aloud, or have a few readers take turns. Then discuss the questions below:

How is the living hope described in verses 3–9 different from hope the world offers? Why does it deserve to be called *living* hope?

Its completely in a person, Jesus Christ.

"Living" because Jesus was raised from the dead.

- Also - or hope is animated. It acts out.

In verses 6–9, Peter says suffering for Jesus shows that our faith is genuine and will lead to joy. Do you find it easy or hard to agree? Explain.

Easy now. Hard when I was younger. I would trade none of my sufferings. They bore more fruit then my times of rejoicing & far more than my times of ease.

In verses 10–12, how does Peter's explanation of the Old Testament give you even more hope?

The OT Prophet were focused on Jesus (without a clear understanding - see Luke 24:26. Wasn't it necessary for Christ to suffer....?

****

Peter's explanation of living hope looks not only to what Jesus has done in the past, but also to what he is doing today and will do in the future. To learn more about this, take turns reading this lesson's article aloud, switching readers at each paragraph break. Then discuss the questions that follow.

ARTICLE

PAST, PRESENT, AND FUTURE GRACE

5 MINUTES

My friend Rob, a pastor in the Pacific Northwest, is passionate about building a gospel culture within his church. To do so, he frequently repeats a mantra to his congregation: "We start with what's right, not with what's wrong."

Like a good gospel minister, Peter starts with what's right. This lesson's passage in 1 Peter is one long sentence in Greek—a sentence full of affirmation and encouragement and hope. To fill us with joy, Peter wants us to draw our attention to the good news of what God has done in the past, the present, and the future.

THE PAST

The resurrection of Jesus Christ from the dead (v. 3) is at the heart of the gospel message. It *happened*—in time and space and history. And that historical, past event has present and future implications.

The resurrection is more than a matter of private religious significance. It's the dawn of a new era, the breaking in of a new kingdom. Christians do not merely believe that Jesus rose from the dead so that our individual sins could be forgiven. We believe that Jesus rose from the dead to renew the whole world. God is putting this broken world back together, and that work decisively began with the resurrection of Jesus.

Have you ever read the Old Testament and felt like you were reading someone else's mail? The prophets can be hard to understand. They use vivid pictures. They speak oracles of woe and judgment. Their messages can seem confusing and obscure. But Peter wants you to remember that this isn't someone else's mail—this is *your* story. Every word God gave his prophets spoke of "the grace that was to be yours" (v. 10).

In light of the resurrection, the message of the Old Testament prophets becomes even clearer. By sending the prophets, God was preparing his people for "the sufferings of Christ and the subsequent glories" (v. 11). Those who "preached the good news to you" (v. 12) were merely completing the story God had begun to tell through the prophets centuries ago.

Think about it: everything God has done in the past has all been building up to this moment. You're here, reading this article, studying this book of the Bible, because centuries ago God made promises to his people. He's fulfilling those promises in and through the work of Jesus. And everyone who belongs to Jesus gets in on those promises.

Even our conversion is a past-tense work of God's grace: "He has caused us to be born again" (v. 3). We didn't change our own hearts. We didn't add up the facts, draw some conclusions, and make a decision for Christ. Yes, we did express faith in Jesus. But our belief is the *outward manifestation* of an internal work of grace. The inner transformation we've experienced is yet another reason to worship and praise and thank God.

THE PRESENT

Many of us, consciously or unconsciously, expect life in the present to be comfortable, safe, and trouble-free. But the Scriptures teach us instead to expect to be "grieved by various trials" (v. 6). Walking with Christ will not be easy. It doesn't exempt us from the hardships of life. But the good news is that these challenges are only "for a little while."

Though Christians may be grieved by various trials, we're also people who "rejoice with joy that is inexpressible" (v. 8) because of our love for the Lord Jesus Christ. Knowing that we belong to Jesus, and he belongs to us, gives us a buoyant and resilient joy as we navigate life on this earth. We have a deep settledness, hard to even express, that endures amid all our pain.

But what about the moments when we feel weak, perplexed, or downcast? In verse 5, Peter reminds his readers that they "by God's power are being guarded through faith."

We tend to think: either I'm doing something, or God's doing it. But what if God is doing it through my doing of it? Pay careful attention to the language of verse 5: "By God's power [you] are being guarded *through* faith." It's not as though God is up there, ruling the universe, and we're down here, just doing our best to hang on. Rather, God is present with us moment-by-moment, sustaining us in faith. We're not passive in the process, but neither are we the determining factor. It's *his* power that guards us. And he guards us by means of our present-tense faith. We hang on to him because he's hanging on to us. This is sweet comfort when we feel our weakness.

THE FUTURE

Many Christians think of salvation as a past-tense event. They look back to some moment in the past when they first believed in Jesus and "got saved." But Peter reminds us that salvation is also forward-looking. Our salvation is something "ready to be revealed in the last time" (v. 5). It's obtained as the outcome of our faith (v. 9). It's something we await, an inheritance that is kept in heaven (v. 4).

If you've ever run a marathon, or made it through a graduate degree, or gone through treatment for a major illness, you know that looking ahead to the future is part of what helps you persevere. The same is true in our life with God. To keep trusting him in the midst of present trials, we need a clear vision of the future glory to come. That's part of what the Holy Spirit is giving us in this text. As your faith matures and grows, you should find yourself anticipating more and more that future day.

And the thing *about* that day that holds the most hope and promise for Christians is "the revelation of Jesus Christ" (v. 7). He's the King we long to see, the glorious Lord we long to behold. Peter reminds us that we have not seen him in the past and that we do not now see him in the present. But one day, we will see him. Our faith will be turned to sight. The love and joy we have now will be eclipsed by an even greater love and joy to come.

CONCLUSION

Human beings tend to have either a past, a present, or a future orientation. Some of us look backward to days gone by, others focus on the here-and-now, and still others are future-oriented visionaries. The amazing thing about the gospel is that it spans all of these time horizons. This past, present, and future hope *is* the good news that has "now been announced to you" (v. 12). The gospel is all of this!

In a world where we're often tempted to look at what's wrong, let's not forget to start with what's right. Let's sink our minds and hearts into this good news into which angels long to look.

DISCUSSION *10 MINUTES*

What things that are going wrong do you spend too much time looking at, and how might you look more at Jesus instead?

When you think of yourself as a Christian, do you have a past, present, or future orientation? How might you benefit from a greater appreciation of all three?

EXERCISE

DYING HOPE VS. LIVING HOPE

20 MINUTES

Our natural tendency is to feel more hopeful when life is going well or when we are pleased with ourselves. But those hopes can dry up. They easily fade and cannot last, so that they are *dying* hopes. The *living* hope Peter describes is entirely different because it's grounded in Jesus's resurrection.

Complete this exercise on your own by reading the descriptions of dying hope and living hope. Circle, underline, or otherwise note some items that sound true of you, or some ways you would like to better realize that Jesus gives you living hope. When you're done, you'll have a chance to share what you noted.

Dying Hope	Living Hope
Rests in cultural influence or political power: "Oh, no! My nation is rejecting the truth."	Rests in Christ's plan and power: "Oh, yes! Jesus is <u>still on his throne.</u>" *and....? go on*
Leads to despair or cynicism: "I can't trust anyone."	Leads to confidence even in troubling times: "I trust Jesus."
Is up to me to sustain: "I must find a reason to carry on and feel hopeful again."	Endures because Christ is alive: "Jesus is not going back in the grave, so he is my True Vine who sustains me." *How?*

Dying Hope	Living Hope
Feels disembodied or distant: "I'll feel better if I can just get in touch with a mystical sense of spiritual peace."	Is real and tangible: "I know I will live with Jesus when he stands again upon a remade earth, and in my flesh I will see God" (see Job 19:25–26).
Remains limited or tainted: "I hope my sin or other troubles don't mess things up this time."	Is unfading and undefiled: "My future is the heavenly city. No enemy can steal it and no sin can stain it" (see Revelation 21:23–27).
Worries about self-performance: "Was I sincere enough when I accepted Jesus? Am I showing God I'm serious enough today?"	Trusts the Savior: "I'm living for Jesus and looking ahead to the salvation he is determined to complete."
Views suffering as a disturbing oddity: "If God is good, this trouble can't be part of his plan for me."	Views suffering as hard, but yet a path to glory: "No trouble in my life will go to waste. God uses it."
Worries that setbacks mean faith is fake. "I've failed God, and now he's against me."	Knows that faith is tested and made genuine through trials: "This crisis shows that God is still pursuing and perfecting me."
Is based on performing for God: "My faith is only as good as my commitment to keep it up."	Is based on Jesus's performance: "My faith itself is evidence of God's work and his unbreakable commitment to me."
Despairs when the times turn evil: "I don't see any way out of this."	Understands that the Bible predicts sufferings and subsequent glories: "This is playing out just the way God said it would."
Leads to restlessness. "Nothing seems to make me really happy."	Leads to settledness and inner joy. "Jesus is with me. I can be calm."

[handwritten margin note: Is there hope in the land of the living? Future only?]

When the group is ready, share and explain some of the differences between dying and living hope that you found meaningful. What items sound true of you today, or were true in the past? How would you like to grow in the future?

WRAP-UP AND PRAYER *10 MINUTES*

As part of your prayer time together, pray that you would know and appreciate the living hope Jesus gives. Also practice having that hope by praying for help to follow Jesus through specific difficulties you face.

3

A HOLY LIFE

BIG IDEA

Our lives as believers should be marked by holiness and love, which fit the goodness of God we have tasted.

BIBLE CONVERSATION *20 MINUTES*

Peter began his letter by reminding us *who we are* and *what we have* in Christ. Now, with that foundation in place, he tells us how these truths transform the way we live. He will refer to a few concepts found throughout the Bible:

- A **holy life** is a pure lifestyle that does not mix with sin or evil, but is set apart to serve God.

- The **fear of God** is a spiritually-healthy trembling that comes when we rightly see our inadequacy in the face of God's majesty. Life's decisions are often driven by fear—fear of loss, of loneliness, of what people will think, etc. Fear of God means that, more than any of these other fears, we shudder to think we might stray from God and his goodness.

Have someone read **1 Peter 1:13–2:3** aloud, or have a few readers take turns. Then discuss the questions below:

What reasons does Peter give for why we should live a holy life? Do people you know think these are *your* reasons for obeying God, or do they think you have other reasons? Explain.

In verse 22 and following, what does a holy life look like? How does this compare to what you and your neighbors usually think when you hear someone say people should be holy?

Based on what Peter has written so far, what are some ways his readers have "tasted that the Lord is good" (2:3)? Have you tasted the same?

* * * *

Now take turns reading this lesson's article aloud, switching readers with each paragraph. Then discuss the questions that follow the article.

ARTICLE

HOLINESS AND LOVE
5 MINUTES

Maybe you've observed that preaching the gospel on a street corner or sharing Christ with a stranger are less welcome than they once were. It's not that the gospel has changed; it's that the culture has. Not so long ago, religious conviction was honored and respected. Now it's more likely to be seen as a sign of bias or bigotry.

In a culture that's skeptical or even hostile toward religion, our conduct matters more than ever. Our neighbors don't just need to *hear* the gospel, they need to *see* how it changes people.

Peter wants to remind us that God's grace does not merely redeem us from sin; it restores us to a life of moral and ethical beauty. So he hones in on two crucial evidences of gospel transformation: *holiness* and *love*. These are the distinct, visible character traits that mark the people of God.

HOLINESS

"As he who called you is holy, you also be holy in all your conduct, since it is written, 'You shall be holy, for I am holy'" (1:15–16). Peter quotes here from the Old Testament book of Leviticus, reminding his readers that holiness is not a new requirement. God has always wanted his people to stand out as distinct from the world, marked by a life of obedience to his ways. And this holiness extends to "all your conduct." In every area of life, Christians must be obedient to the Lord. The cultural values and practices they went along with before they came to know Jesus must be set aside. As God is, so must his people be.

What animates the pursuit of holiness? First, holiness is fueled by our new family identity. Notice the adoption motif: obedient children (v. 14) calling on their Father (v. 17). We belong to God. He is our Father. He loves us, and he's helping us and encouraging us and spurring us on toward holiness. He rejoices as we take on the family resemblance, bearing his image more and more.

Second, holiness is fueled by the fear of God: "Conduct yourselves with fear throughout the time of your exile" (v. 17). Being mindful of the glory and honor that God rightly deserves—and meditating on the beauty of his holiness—motivates us to become holy as he is holy.

Third, holiness is fueled by remembering the price of our redemption. We were redeemed not with "perishable things such as silver or gold, but with the precious blood of Christ" (vv. 18–19). Jesus died for us! Knowing what he gave to make us his own, why would we not want to live for him?

LOVE

Holiness without love can seem separatist and puritanical. And love without holiness can seem mushy and sentimental. But love and holiness together are a powerful force. What might the world conclude if they saw a people so committed to holiness that nothing could make them compromise, and so committed to love that nothing could make them defensive? That's the kind of people God is out to create, by his grace. He wants Christians to be marked by a kind of love that's counter-cultural and distinct.

First, he commands us in this passage to "love one another earnestly" (v. 22). The word here means "unremittingly, continually, intensely." Real Christian love never pulls back, never gives up, never wavers. It's as though the switch is always on.

Second, he commands us to love "from a pure heart." The word *kardia* ("heart") literally means "from the guts" or "with everything in you." It's a straining-forward, all-in kind of love that pushes through apathy and hurt feelings and relational slights.

We can't love this way unless we've been born again (v. 23). And if we *have* been born again, then the imperishable seed of the gospel is growing and bearing fruit in our hearts. God's grace is at work in us, day by day and moment by moment, overcoming our selfishness, healing our brokenness, and strengthening us in our weakness. The progress may seem slow, arduous, even imperceptible at times, but it's happening.

As we continue in "obedience to the truth" (v. 22), our virtue grows and our love is strengthened. This is how gospel transformation happens: by grit and by grace. It's not "let go and let God," nor is it "God helps those who help themselves." It's (1) God's work of new birth through his living and abiding word, resulting in (2) our willful obedience to the truth. It's God setting us apart as holy, with the result that we strive to be holy in all our conduct.

So, Christian: put away (actively choose to reject) malice and deceit and hypocrisy and envy and slander. These sins break relationships, destroy community, and undermine Christian love. Wherever they are present in your conduct, put them to death. Instead, indulge your craving for the things of God, like a hungry infant longing for milk. Since you've tasted of his goodness, hunger for more of him.

CONCLUSION

Peter is telling us to reject truncated versions of the gospel: "gospels" of eternal salvation that have no bearing on our lives now, or "gospels" of social activism that minimize the need to be born again. The only gospel worth believing is the glorious good news of God's redeeming, sanctifying, transforming grace, which both causes us to be born again and helps us grow up into salvation.

Sin has led us into moral ugliness; Jesus restores us to moral beauty. Sin has made us selfish and cynical; Jesus restores our capacity to love. Where you find holiness and love among God's people, there you will always find the genuine gospel of grace.

DISCUSSION *10 MINUTES*

Where have you noticed that people don't just need to hear the gospel, but need to see how it changes you?

Which faulty approach to the Christian life do you most often fall into? Explain.

- "Just be yourself." (neglecting to strive for holiness)
- "Just try harder." (thinking it's all up to you to prove how holy you are)

3

EXERCISE

CHANGING YOUR APPETITE

20 MINUTES

A common misunderstanding of holiness is that it means you have to say no to many things you want to do and yes to things that are less fun. But while it's true that resisting sin takes discipline (since sin often feels good in the moment), holiness grows from seeing that God is better. To use Peter's analogy of taste: you change your appetite. Having tasted that the Lord is good, you long for pure spiritual milk—for a holy life. You find that it satisfies in a way your old diet of sin and self-love couldn't.

The diagram on the next page shows that the process is circular: a taste of God's goodness leads to a craving for more and a changed appetite, but holy living reveals more "unhealthy eating" in your life, and this drives you to taste again still more of God's better nourishment. On your own, read through the diagram. Note parts that seem true of your life and where in the circle you feel you are today. Then fill in some details in the second, blank diagram (you don't have to fill in every square). You'll discuss your responses later.

Tasting that the Lord Is Good.

Freedom from worldly fears and cravings begins with tasting God's goodness. Taste is experienced: you don't just profess to be ransomed by Christ's blood, you *take it in.* You more deeply feel your Savior's love. You resample the honor of serving his kingdom. You catch a whiff of how satisfying it is to have God working in you.

Seeing Your Unhealthy Diet.

Holy living is hard. Your regimen of loving others (as you put away malice, deceit, hypocrisy, envy, and slander) will reveal how much you're still driven by the world's fears and enticed by its "artificial sweeteners," which can't really satisfy your cravings. You feel a renewed need for God.

Craving More of God.

A taste grows into a craving. Your old hungers (for worldly approval, influence, comforts, physical pleasures, intimacy) no longer satisfy. You start to desire the comforts and purposes found in Jesus instead. Your new cravings for a pure and spiritual life push out the old ones.

Changing Your Appetite.

You come to realize that you were made to feast on God's love and to enjoy serving him in all you do. Self-interest starts to taste phony or sour, while love for others tastes genuine and sweet. You experience holy living—the transforming power of the imperishable, life-giving Word of the Lord.

Tasting that the Lord Is Good.
How have you sampled the
comfort of Jesus's blood,
the thrill of his work in you,
or the honor of serving
his kingdom?

**Seeing Your
Unhealthy Diet.**
What worldly fears supplant
a healthy fear of God in you,
hindering your love? What
worldly cravings often tempt you?

Craving More of God.
What new and holy cravings
are supplanting old and sinful
ones in you? What more of
God do you desire?

Changing Your Appetite.
What have you come to truly
enjoy about giving up
self-interest, living for God, and
sincerely loving others?

When the group is ready, share some of your responses. What have you tasted of God, and how is your appetite for a holy life changing? Where in the circle diagram have you recently been, or where do you feel you are now (you might be in more than one spot at once)?

WRAP-UP AND PRAYER *10 MINUTES*

Most diets require healthy habits to maintain, and it's the same with spiritual growth. One helpful habit is to regularly pray, both on your own and with others, for God to give you tastes of his goodness and cravings for a holy life. Take time now to pray for both yourself and others in your group.

4

JESUS THE CORNERSTONE

BIG IDEA

We are not meant to be isolated believers, but a connected people whose honor and core identity is built on Jesus.

BIBLE CONVERSATION *20 MINUTES*

In this lesson's passage from 1 Peter, the apostle quotes or alludes to seven other Bible passages: Exodus 19, Psalm 34, Psalm 118, Isaiah 8, Isaiah 28, Isaiah 43, and Hosea 2. In doing so, Peter not only gives us a lesson in how to read the whole Bible, but continues writing about what it means that we are Jesus's people. Peter uses each reference creatively and intentionally to show how Jesus satisfies the promises and prophecies of the Old Testament. The temple, the priesthood, the sacrifices, the covenants, the holy city—all of these find their fulfillment in Jesus and his people.

This lesson's article will explain the Old Testament connections. For now, think about the images Peter evokes and what they mean, realizing that in ancient times a building's cornerstone would be carefully selected to provide critical stability for the entire structure. Have someone read **1 Peter 2:4–10** aloud, and then discuss the questions below:

What are some ways this passage says Jesus and his people are similar? What do you like about the imagery Peter uses to say this?

How does Peter's view of what deserves honor and shame differ from what people you know might say?

In verses 9 and 10, to what purpose has Jesus called his people? How does this differ from other ways you've thought of your purpose in life as a group of believers?

****

Now read the article aloud, taking turns by paragraph, to learn more about the meaning behind Peter's imagery. Then discuss the questions that follow.

4

ARTICLE

JESUS AND HIS PEOPLE

5 MINUTES

As people shaped by individualism and consumerism, we desperately need a stronger conviction about the priority of the church. We tend to view the church as something nice rather than as something necessary. But Peter wants to show us that good *ecclesiology* (a healthy doctrine of the church) starts with good *Christology* (a right understanding of Jesus). He wants us to see *who Jesus is* so we can better understand *who we are*—and why we need one another. The passage makes four main points about Jesus and his church.

1. Jesus is the cornerstone, and therefore the church is built on him. When King David wanted to build a temple to house the ark of God, the Lord told him not to: "The LORD declares to you that the LORD will make you a house. When your days are fulfilled and you lie down with your fathers, I will raise up your offspring after you, who shall come from your body, and I will establish his kingdom" (2 Samuel 7:11–12). David intended to build God a physical house, but God turned the language in a metaphorical direction. He promised to build David a dynasty, a kingdom. Central to this promise was a descendant who would come from David's line.

This Davidic descendant is also hinted at in Psalm 118, which the Jewish people sung at Passover: "The stone that the builders rejected has become the cornerstone. This is the LORD's doing; it is marvelous in our eyes" (vv. 22–23). In the years between the Old and New Testaments, rabbinic tradition had identified this stone as the Messiah. So Peter is gathering up all this stone imagery and bringing it together. In Jesus, God is finally building his house—the very kingdom he promised to David.

Jesus is the cornerstone, and everyone who comes to Jesus becomes a living stone in that great building project. The church is built upon Jesus. It's not defined by who shows up at a building or who participates in a worship service. It's defined by those who come to Jesus and build their lives on him, and we should long for more and more people to do just that.

2. Jesus is the living stone, and therefore the church is connected in him. By itself, a brick is merely a brick. But as many bricks are built together by a wise mason, they form a beautiful and complex structure. Likewise, Peter reminds us, "You yourselves like living stones are being built up as a spiritual house" (v. 5).

A house is something bigger, more imposing, and more impressive than its individual stones. Jesus isn't out to gather a mound of scattered stones. He's out to build a house, a temple, a glorious cathedral. And he's saved you to fit you into that structure.

There's no room, then, for a "me and Jesus" Christianity that neglects your connection to the rest of the stones in God's spiritual house. You are meant to be part of the church. Your well-being is caught up with the well-being of the church. You can't become who you're meant to be apart from the church, and the church can't be all it's intended to be without you.

3. Jesus is the stumbling stone, and therefore the church will be rejected like him. In verses 7 and 8, Peter blends cornerstone imagery from Psalm 118 and stumbling-stone imagery from Isaiah 8. Jesus, who gives a stable identity for our lives and for the church, is at the same time a stumbling stone and a rock of offense to many.

New Testament scholar Leonhard Goppelt puts it this way: "Christ is laid across the path of humanity on its course into the future. In the encounter with him each person is changed: one for salvation, another for destruction. . . . One cannot simply step over Jesus to go on about the daily routine and pass him by to build a future. . . . Either one sees and becomes 'a living stone,' or one stumbles as a blind person over Christ and comes to ruin."[3]

Jesus won't get out of the way. God has laid him across the path of humanity. You have to do something with him.

In our day and age, many stumble over Jesus. And because they don't like him, they don't like his people either. Though we may be shamed by the culture around us, God promises that we who believe in Jesus will not be put to shame. By contrast, those who seek the world's honor by rejecting Christ will ultimately come to shame as they face the righteous judgment of God.

Since you're going to be rejected and shamed for your faith in Jesus, don't go it alone. You're meant to be part of a community where you can experience the honor that Christ bestows on his people.

4. Jesus is the true Israel, and therefore the church is united in him. In verses 9 and 10, Peter uses four terms drawn from Isaiah 43 and Exodus 19. In their original context, these words were spoken "to the people of Israel" (Exodus 19:6). But Peter applies them to both Jews and Gentiles who had responded to the gospel message and embraced Jesus in faith. In doing so, he reminds us that God's chosen people are no longer defined by ethnic lineage, but by spiritual lineage. Jesus is the head of God's new-covenant people.

The terms *chosen race, royal priesthood, holy nation*, and *people for his own possession* are all communal terms. No individual is a race unto himself, and no single person can be a nation. To be called to Jesus is to be brought into a *people*. And that people exists for a purpose: "that you may proclaim the excellencies of him who called you out of darkness into his marvelous light" (v. 9). The church, as God's community, exists to display and declare his glory to a watching world.

These four points show that being united to Jesus means being united to his church. Jesus is the cornerstone of a great spiritual house, the high priest of a royal priesthood, and the leader of a new people drawn from every tribe and tongue and nation. If your view of Jesus is small, your view of the church will likely be small as well. But once you see Jesus rightly, you'll gain a whole new vision for the significance of his church—and you'll be committed to its flourishing.

DISCUSSION *10 MINUTES*

How have you experienced the connectivity of God's people, where how you are doing spiritually affects others and how they are doing affects you?

When your culture suggests it's shameful to be a believer, how does being in a community of believers help you?

Lesson

EXERCISE

4

WHAT'S YOUR FOUNDATION?

20 MINUTES

Did you notice how Peter keeps using the word *believe* as he writes about Jesus being your cornerstone—your foundation in life? To Peter, there's no such thing as a believer for whom Jesus is just another "stone" among many influences. Rather, a believer is someone for whom Jesus is *the* core identity on which their whole life is built.

Even if you know this, other identities might take over your thinking and threaten to be the functional foundation of your life. In this exercise, work on your own to notice competing foundations in your life and how Jesus is better. After you've completed both parts below, you'll share some of your responses with the group.

PART 1: Worldly identities. Begin by reading through this list of common places you might find your core, controlling identity other than having Jesus as your life's foundation.

Possible Core Identities in Life

Work or career	Political leaders or causes
Family (immediate or extended)	Ideological convictions
Personal skills/abilities	Social causes or activism
Achievements or notoriety	National or ethnic heritage
Health commitments or lifestyle	Theological/church distinctives
Acquired possessions	Community or school loyalties
Social circles	Sports teams

Now ask yourself four questions that help reveal which identities you're treating as the core of who you are. For each question below, pick a few identities from the list above (or write your own answer that better fits how you tend to identify).

Proclaiming. Peter says believers proclaim the excellencies of Jesus. What things from the list do you tend to praise, draw attention to, or talk about instead? _____

_____

_____

_____

_____

Shame and honor. Peter says shame or honor is found in your response to Jesus. What things from the list are more likely to make you feel either good about yourself or ashamed? _____

_____

_____

_____

_____

Community. Peter says your core community is built around Jesus and his people. What things from the list form other communities that feel more important to you? _____

_____

_____

_____

_____

Sacrifice. Peter says your life is one of offering spiritual sacrifices through Jesus. What things from the list are you likely to sacrifice your time, money, health, etc. for instead? _____

_____

_____

_____

_____

PART 2: Jesus as your core identity. Happily, there's a second list. The path to living out the true core identity you have in Jesus begins with believing the gospel. And already in his letter, Peter has reminded you of several gospel truths that make Jesus a more satisfying foundation for who you are. So now, read through that list.

Reasons Jesus Is the Best Core Identity

He is alive forever, lasting and unfading (1:3–4).

He is undefiled and perfect (1:4).

He changes you into a genuine, tested, honor-worthy person (1:6–7).

He will lovingly save your soul rather than suck it dry (1:8–9).

He is relevant in all times and all places (1:10–12).

He was devoted to you first, ransoming you with his blood (1:18–19).

He gives a hope that is sure in God, not iffy in this world (1:21).

He creates pure love in you instead of indulging self-interest (1:22).

He gives new life by his word that never dies (1:23–25).

He gives true, certain, heavenly honor (2:6–7).

He has called you out of darkness into light that is marvelous (2:9).

In him you belong not to any created thing, but to God himself (2:10).

His heart is not to demand from you, but to show mercy to you (2:10).

Now consider again the worldly identities that tend to control you. Which of Peter's truths about Jesus (which your worldly identities can't offer) most encourage you to make Jesus your foundation in life? _____

_____

_____

_____

_____

When the group is ready, share some of your responses. Do you see any patterns? What things tend to feel like a foundational identity to you, and how is Jesus a better cornerstone?

WRAP-UP AND PRAYER *10 MINUTES*

As part of your prayer time together, you might ask God to help you make Jesus the cornerstone of your lives and to draw you closer to each other in helpful community. You might also reread Peter's description of who you are in verses 9 and 10, and thank God for what he has made you as a people.

Lesson

5

FOLLOWING IN JESUS'S STEPS

BIG IDEA

The chief way to bring glory to God in an ungodly society is not to fight against it but to do good within it, following the example of Jesus.

BIBLE CONVERSATION *20 MINUTES*

Having said that believers are a distinct people, Peter moves on to tell his readers how they should live within Greco-Roman society. Peter will mention several relationships found in that culture's power structures: wives with their husbands, household servants with their masters, and citizens with the imperial government (which may have had outbursts of brutality toward Christians by this time).

As you read, notice that Peter neither condones nor condemns the way these relationships worked in that culture. Instead, you will see throughout the passage a whole different way to subvert any society: winning over unbelievers through good and gentle behavior rather than giving in to passion-driven behavior, even when mistreated. The society in which you live surely differs from ancient Greco-Roman culture in both good and bad ways, but try to take Peter's words as instruction for your heart rather than as a blueprint for society-building.

Have someone read **1 Peter 2:11–3:7** aloud, or have several readers take turns. Then discuss the questions below:

List several principles Peter gives for living under authority. Which would you find difficult, and why? What wisdom do you see in them?

Verse 21 says to follow in Christ's steps. What are the *motives* behind this behavior, and what are the *goals* of this kind of life?

Wives are told to prize inner beauty above outward appearances. How might that same instruction fit everyone Peter addresses here (citizens, servants, husbands), and your own station in life as well?

****

Next, take turns by paragraph reading the article aloud, and then discuss the questions at the end.

Lesson

ARTICLE

5

AN ALTERNATE SOCIETY

5 MINUTES

When I was a teenager, I participated in an evangelism training program at my church. The leaders taught us a simple, five-point outline for sharing the gospel message. Then they sent us out in teams to visit newcomers to the church and walk them through a gospel presentation.

To this day, I think every Christian should be equipped to share the gospel verbally with another person. However, the model of evangelism I learned in my home church assumed that people had a basic concept of God's existence, some level of familiarity with the Bible, and a baseline respect for church workers. Tim Keller refers to this kind of evangelism as "rearranging the furniture." It assumes people already have the right ideas and concepts in their minds. We just need to rearrange things so that they see their sin and their need for Christ.

But what if they don't have the furniture in the first place? Peter is writing to Christians living in a skeptical—and even hostile—culture. Reaching their neighbors will require more than rearranging the furniture. It will require long-term, life-on-life engagement that shows the gospel's impact on every area of life.

IN HIS STEPS

Living a life devoted to God in the midst of a culture that doesn't understand such things will open us up to ridicule, slander, and even persecution. The center of this lesson's passage focuses on Jesus as our model and example. Our job is to follow in his steps (v. 21) and entrust ourselves to God who judges justly (v. 23).

Peter borrows imagery and words from Isaiah 53 to remind us that Jesus is the Suffering Servant. His followers must be ready to suffer as he did. It was Jesus's humility, gentleness, and trust in suffering that set him apart. Likewise, as Christians endure sorrow and suffering with patience and joy, we will stand out in a world driven by self-interest.

Working outward from this basic exhortation to follow in Jesus's steps, Peter focuses on the gospel's implications for key relationships that were of particular interest in his day. Unbelievers would be judging Christians by whether they could be a stable part of society, complying with the expectations of a typical Greco-Roman household. Peter affirms this to a point, but gives it a gospel twist that will end up reshaping that culture more than any outright opposition might.[4]

In all these areas of society, Christians are to *do good*—a phrase Peter uses in 2:15, 2:20, and 3:6. For citizens, doing good means honoring and submitting to the authority of the state. For household servants, doing good means respecting and honoring their masters. For wives, doing good means submitting to their husbands. And for husbands, doing good means living with their wives in an understanding and gentle way. Through their virtuous behavior in all these spheres, Christians will "silence the ignorance of foolish people" (2:15).

WAIT ... REALLY?

Reading these instructions in our day raises a host of questions. Are we to submit even to oppressive governments? If our servitude is forced, is it okay to seek freedom? Aren't there times when a wife should *not* submit to her husband? You're probably aware of situations where Peter's words have been twisted to condone violence, oppression, and subjugation. But two quotes from Karen Jobes's book on 1 Peter help us see that far from justifying a sinful status quo, Peter has a much deeper gospel subversion in mind:

> When read within its original historical setting, these verses become a call to social transformation within the Christian community, allowing it to become an alternate society based on God's redemptive plan.[5]

> The call to follow the crucified Messiah was, in the long run, much more effective in changing the unjust political, economic, and familial structures than direct exhortations to revolutionize them would ever have been. For an allegiance to the crucified Messiah—indeed, worship of a crucified God—is an eminently political act that subverts a politics of dominion at its very core.[6]

Remember, Peter is teaching us how to live as gospel witnesses. He envisions the church as an *alternate society*. Christians have the same life situations as the people around us: we are citizens, we are employees or employers, we are husbands and wives and parents and children. Yet in each of these areas, we live with Christian distinctiveness. How we conduct ourselves in each of these spheres gives opportunity for the people around us to see our good deeds and glorify God (2:12). In a culture that doesn't have the gospel furniture to comprehend a basic gospel presentation, our conduct becomes a key part of our evangelistic strategy.

It's no accident that Peter begins this whole section of the book by reminding his readers again that they are exiles (2:11). In fact, he uses the phrase "sojourners and exiles," the same words Abraham used to describe himself in Genesis.* Abraham and Sarah are models of life in exile. They were called by God to leave their home and go to a new land. They chose to worship the one true God in contrast to the pagan society around them. They learned to trust God, even when doing so was contrary to cultural expectations. In challenging situations, they had to do good and not fear anything that was frightening (3:6).

Like Abraham and Sarah, we are called to a counter-cultural existence. The way we live won't immediately make sense to people who don't share our convictions. But over time, as they see our honorable conduct, they will be provoked to ask deeper questions about the God we worship. And when they do, we'll have the opportunity to talk about the Savior who "bore our sins in his body on the tree, that we might die to sin and live to righteousness" (2:24).

DISCUSSION *10 MINUTES*

What role does doing good have in your Christian witness, and how might you give it a larger role?

When you are suffering unjustly, how does that affect your efforts to live a good life? Does doing good become easier or harder for you? More or less important?

---

* Genesis 23:4

5

EXERCISE

JESUS'S EXAMPLE AND HIS CROSS

20 MINUTES

It can be hard to follow Jesus's example, especially when that means suffering. But Peter doesn't only say Jesus is our example; he also shows us Jesus's finished work on the cross. These go together: the cross keeps the command to follow Jesus from being a guilty burden, and Jesus's example reminds us not to think of the cross as a free pass to sin, but as power to overcome sin.

For this exercise, you'll work on your own to read again what Peter says about Jesus—both his example and his cross—and consider what it means to your life. At the end, you'll share some of your responses with the group.

JESUS'S EXAMPLE. Underline or otherwise note parts of the Bible passage or the reflections below (vv. 22–23) that you find especially meaningful as you think about following Jesus's example. (Note what sounds extra difficult, or makes you appreciate Jesus better, or helps you understand the Christian life, etc.)

"He committed no sin, neither was deceit found in his mouth."
Jesus's example begins with being completely true and selfless in

everything he has done, including every word he has ever spoken, no matter what the circumstance.

"When he was reviled, he did not revile in return . . ." Even when people unfairly blamed, criticized, and made fun of him, Jesus never did the same to them.

"when he suffered, he did not threaten . . ." Even though Jesus rightly could have punished, then and there, everyone responsible for his death, he chose to keep submitting and even prayed for the soldiers who crucified him.

"but continued entrusting himself to him who judges justly." In all of this, Jesus never doubted or resented God's plan for him, but drew closer to God for constant support, believing God would glorify him through suffering and make all things right in the end.

JESUS'S CROSS. Again, underline or otherwise note some parts of the Bible passage or the reflections below (vv. 24–25) that you find especially meaningful or encouraging.

"He himself bore our sins in his body on the tree . . ." The world's only sinless person (the one who never deserved to die or suffer or be ashamed of anything) left the praises of heaven to suffer and die in your place, cursed and shamed on the cross as he wore your sin—so you are fully forgiven when you fail.

"that we might die to sin and live to righteousness." Jesus's suffering in your place kills off sin's power over you: you are no longer counted guilty, headed for punishment, or destined for shame, and you have God's strength to resist sin in your life and to act with godly honor.

"By his wounds you have been healed." The damaging hostility that your sin created between you and God is mended, and today you are able to enjoy life with God—a healing that will last forever and become perfect.

"For you were straying like sheep, but have now returned to the Shepherd and Overseer of your souls." You have a home with the heavenly Father and faithful Brother you have always needed. Jesus will forever guard you, guide you, comfort you, listen to you, stay near to you, and seat you at his table.

THE EXAMPLE AND THE CROSS TOGETHER. Now think about how some of the phrases you picked from the EXAMPLE section interact with those from the CROSS section. How does knowing one section encourage you in the other, or add richness to the other, etc.? You might write down a few thoughts as you wait for the group to finish.

When the group is ready, share some of your responses. What did you notice, and why?

Peter addressed key relationships within his Greco-Roman society, but what about *your* society? Think of an important relationship that's been a struggle for you. How might Jesus's *example* and his cross—both of them together—encourage you to do good in that situation?

WRAP-UP AND PRAYER *10 MINUTES*

In your prayer time together, include prayers for your relationships and for the courage and desire to follow in Jesus's steps.

6

SEEKING PEACE

BIG IDEA

A life of humble love will please God and bring us blessings, even if we suffer, and is possible because Christ first suffered for us.

BIBLE CONVERSATION *20 MINUTES*

Peter has been explaining the redemption we've received in Jesus and the humble, suffering way Jesus won it for us. He says this should reshape the way we live in this world which will, in turn, be a powerful witness about Jesus even though we are denounced as exiles here.

In this lesson's passage, Peter will continue this theme by building around Psalm 34, a song that celebrates the wisdom of humbly trusting God, seeking to do good, and being poor in spirit. Have someone read **1 Peter 3:8–18** aloud, or have a few readers take turns. Then discuss the questions below:

Look at the strategy presented in verses 8–12. How is it different from most people's strategy for success in life, or from yours?

In verses 13–18, what are the main things to consider when you have to explain why you believe in Jesus? How do they compare to what you typically think about in that situation?

What truths will you have to believe about Jesus if you're going to dare to live the way this passage suggests? Explain.

* * * *

Now read the article, "Breaking the Evil-for-Evil Cycle." Take turns by paragraph reading it aloud, and then discuss the questions that follow.

Lesson

ARTICLE

BREAKING THE EVIL-FOR-EVIL CYCLE

5 MINUTES

At the heart of every conflict, from marital strife to workplace discord to full-scale global war, is the evil-for-evil cycle. It works like this: someone treats you poorly, and you respond in kind.

Returning evil for evil is such a basic human problem that it shows up among the youngest children. It happens on the playground. It happens among neighbors. It happens in the boardroom. It happens in the halls of government. And with the rise of social media, it happens online—perhaps more frequently than anywhere else.

If our human relationships are going to display true beauty, the cycle is going to have to be broken. Someone is going to have to choose *not* to repay evil for evil or insult for insult. And that someone was Jesus.

What's more, if you are saved by Jesus, Peter says that someone should now be *you*. Every day, in every conflict, you can choose to retaliate or you can choose to "turn away from evil and do good" (v. 11). Jesus came and broke the pattern, and now the gospel sets Christians free to break the evil-for-evil cycle in our relationships too, just like him.

WHAT DRIVES THE CYCLE?

Why are we so quick to strike back when others speak evil against us? Quite simply, hostile speech triggers our desire to be vindicated. If someone has spoken falsely about us, we want to make the truth known. If someone harms our reputation, we want to defend ourselves. If someone has wrongly judged us, we want to set the record straight. To say it another way: we want to be *justified*.

But this is exactly the need Jesus has met for us. As Peter puts it, "Christ also suffered once for sins, the righteous for the unrighteous, that he might bring us to God" (v. 18). Jesus was righteous, holy, unblemished. He suffered in our place—took upon himself our unrighteousness. We've already *been* vindicated. Our sins have been paid for. A new identity has been given to us. Before God, our reputation is clean and our status is secure.

Resting in this truth is what gives us the power to endure evil and reviling and slander. We don't have to strike back. We don't *need* to defend ourselves or justify ourselves or make sure the truth is known. God knows all. His eyes are on the righteous, and we belong to him through Jesus.

But it's not just the *what* of the gospel that helps us break the evil-for-evil cycle. It's also the *how* of the gospel. In accomplishing our salvation, Jesus suffered *as a righteous person*. Unjust suffering is at the heart of the gospel message! It's the means by which Jesus conquered sin. Knowing *that* we've been vindicated frees us from the need to defend ourselves. And knowing *how* we've been vindicated inspires us to follow our Savior's example.

As Karen Jobes points out, "It is exactly when we are insulted and treated with malicious intent that we are most tempted to respond in kind. . . . Those who are able not simply to clench their teeth and remain silent but to maintain an inner attitude that allows one to pray sincerely for the well-being of one's adversaries, are truly a witness to the life-changing power of a new identity in Christ."[7]

THE EFFECT OF BREAKING THE CYCLE

Returning blessing for evil will certainly bring greater peace to our friendships, our marriages, and our churches. But the Holy Spirit has an even bigger end in mind. Breaking the evil-for-evil cycle has an impact on our enemies and on our own consciences.

According to verse 16, blessing those who curse us causes our enemies to be put to shame. Slander, reviling, and verbal hostility are attempts to shame others—to dishonor, demean, or discredit them. But as God's people respond to this attempted shaming with blessing and love and peace, the dynamics of shame are reversed. The bullies are put to shame, and the peacemakers are honored.

It's easy to see examples of this throughout history. The early Christians, though reviled and slandered by the society around them, cared for the Roman poor and took in abandoned children. These merciful actions caused fourth-century emperor Julian the Apostate to admit: "These impious Galileans not only feed their own poor, but ours also!" Hugh Latimer and Nicholas Ridley were burned at the stake in Oxford in 1555, and their peace and prayerfulness in martyrdom lit the torch of the Protestant Reformation throughout England. Corrie Ten Boom endured great hostility from the Nazis in a concentration camp, but history lauds her and condemns her persecutors. In the moment, turning the other cheek seems weak and foolish and unheroic. But over time, the world notices and God is glorified.

Breaking the evil-for-evil cycle also blesses our own consciences. Imagine the feeling of a totally clean conscience: no hidden sin, no unresolved burdens, no nagging moral doubts—just the pure feeling of mental rest and spiritual peace. A good conscience, as

Peter calls it in verse 16, is the basis of real confidence before God and others. When we know we have nothing to hide and nothing to fear, we'll find ourselves praying like David in Psalm 26, "Vindicate me, O LORD, for I have walked in my integrity." David was a sinner, but he was a repentant sinner with a clear conscience before the Lord. And you can be too.

Peter tells us to be ready to talk about Jesus to anyone who asks. But *why* would anyone ask us about the hope that is in us? The text suggests it's because they see us not repaying evil for evil. They see our zeal for what is good. They see us suffering for righteousness' sake. Breaking the evil-for-evil cycle is so counter-cultural, so unusual, so different from normal human behavior, that it demands an explanation.

To say it another way, applying the gospel to our own hearts generates the opportunity to proclaim the gospel to others. So let's start with ourselves. Let's believe the gospel deeply enough to reject defensiveness and retaliation and payback. And let's allow the good news to overflow from our own hearts into the lives of others.

DISCUSSION *10 MINUTES*

Payback often feels good in the moment. But tell about a time you felt a greater pleasure because you resisted payback, and broke the evil-for-evil cycle.

The article mentioned three effects of breaking the evil-for-evil cycle: (1) peace among believers, (2) honor in the world, and (3) a good conscience before God. Which do you especially long for, and why?

Lesson

6

EXERCISE

SPEECH AND THE GOSPEL

20 MINUTES

You naturally want to be respected and right. This means that defensiveness and paybacks happen instinctively. They will be impossible for you to overcome unless, as the article said, you deeply know that you already *are* right. This gospel assurance and rest is part of Jesus's power to transform you.

Like Peter's letter, this exercise will focus on how you speak, since words reveal what's in your heart. Each item below contains three elements:

1. A sinful way of **speech** that might be how you often talk.
2. A **need** your heart feels that fuels your sinful speech.
3. The **gospel** answer that tells how your need is already met, or replaced with something better, in Jesus. Like Peter, each gospel answer will use a part of Psalm 34 to encourage you about Jesus.

Read through each item on your own. Note some ways of speaking that tend to be true of you, and ponder the gospel answers to the

64

needs you feel. When the group is ready, discuss the questions at the end of the exercise.

Speech: Gossip, mockery, criticism

Need: "I need to think I'm more right than others."

Gospel: You are already perfectly right with God—where it counts. At the cross, Jesus took all your unrighteousness on himself, and now he gives you his flawless righteousness. "None of those who take refuge in him will be condemned" (Psalm 34:22).

Speech: Defensiveness, blame-shifting, excuse-making, downplaying my faults

Need: "I need for others to think I'm alright."

Gospel: You already have respect. Jesus fully took the shame of your sin on himself when he died for you. In him, you enjoy heavenly dignity even though you still sin at times, and it's actually honor-building to admit this. "Those who look to him are radiant, and their faces shall never be ashamed" (Psalm 34:5).

Speech: Bragging, talking about myself

Need: "I need to be noticed, appreciated, or celebrated."

Gospel: You already are appreciated. Your heavenly Father delights in you as his child, just as he delights in *the* Son. Jesus and his spotless record have become *your* reputation, giving you something really worth boasting about. "My soul makes its boast in the Lord; let the humble hear and be glad" (Psalm 34:2).

Speech: Backbiting, vindictive talk

Need: "I need justice."

Gospel: Justice is already coming. Jesus will dispense perfect and unselfish justice everywhere it's right to do so. What's more, in the cross, his justice is joined with mercy for many—starting with you! "The face of the Lord is against those who do evil, to cut off the memory of them from the earth" (Psalm 34:16).

Speech: Complaining, demandingness

Need: "I need to get what I want."

Gospel: You already have your soul's true longing—God himself—and a heavenly inheritance that cannot fade or be defiled and is more precious than gold. "Those who seek the Lord lack no good thing" (Psalm 34:10).

Speech: Backtalk, insisting on the last word

Need: "I need to win."

Gospel: Jesus has already won where it counts. He is destined to defeat every untruth, banish every evil, end death forever, and fully vindicate you for your faith in him. "The angel of the Lord encamps around those who fear him, and delivers them" (Psalm 34:7).

Speech: Flattery, saying whatever people want to hear

Need: "I need to please others, or earn intimacy."

Gospel: You already have the best intimacy: a nearness to God that you can never lose. He gives your heart true comfort and love.

"The Lord is near to the brokenhearted and saves the crushed in spirit" (Psalm 34:18).

Speech: Rash or harsh talk, eagerness to scold

Need: "I need to feel angry."

Gospel: Your bigger problem with anger has already been turned on its head. God's rightful wrath *against you* was absorbed by Jesus on the cross, making the theme of your life one where mercy overcomes hostility, frustration, and tears. "This poor man cried, and the Lord heard him and saved him" (Psalm 34:6).

Speech: Deception, lies

Need: "More than I need truth, I need all these other needs to be met."

Gospel: All your real needs are already met in Jesus, and this lets you be truthful. The truth of the gospel is your constant need: it sets you free from the fear of what people might think and what the world might do, letting you serve God and genuinely love others. "I sought the Lord, and he answered me and delivered me from all my fears" (Psalm 34:4).

Other: _____
_____
_____

Discuss: Which speech behaviors are especially true of you, and what gospel answers do you find helpful? Explain.

Have you tried other methods to control your tongue (perhaps willpower, self-scolding, learning from consequences, etc.)? How might more fully believing the gospel bring deeper change in you than those other methods could?

WRAP-UP AND PRAYER *10 MINUTES*

Prayer is a way to exercise your belief in the gospel, so it's an important element in gospel-based growth. Pray together that God would help you live the way Peter describes in his letter.

Lesson

7

THE RIGHTEOUS CONQUEROR

BIG IDEA

When we get discouraged or doubt that God intends to be good to us, we should look to Jesus. He is the righteous Savior who died for us and the conqueror of every power that threatens to keep us from God.

BIBLE CONVERSATION *15 MINUTES*

This lesson's Bible passage will include two lines that often cause readers to be confused or ask questions:

1. Peter writes that Jesus, along with dying and rising again, also "went and proclaimed to the spirits in prison" (v. 19) who had disobeyed in Noah's day. It is unlikely that Peter means Jesus preached the gospel in hell or offered salvation to the dead, since the Bible suggests this does not happen.* But through the Spirit, Jesus has preached all over creation, beginning already in Old Testament times (as Peter pointed out in 1:10–12). And Jesus's victory is proclaimed to all sorts of human and spiritual creatures "in heaven and

---

* See Matthew 25:41–46; Luke 16:25–26; Hebrews 9:27

on earth and under the earth,"* reminding us that unseen realms exist. Peter's wording may suggest Jesus visited a domain of death, but the point is to see Jesus's triumph over every domain of both life and death, mysterious as some of these realms remain to us.

2. Peter writes that baptism "now saves you." At first glance, this might seem to conflict with the Bible's teaching that we are saved only by Jesus, through faith in him. But in this passage Peter also points out that indeed it is the inward reality of faith rather than the outward washing that saves us. This should keep us from taking a "checklist" approach to salvation that relies on completing external steps like baptism; we are to rely only on Jesus. But baptism publicly joins us to our Savior and his people. For the persecuted believers in Peter's world, the inward decision of faith to follow Jesus would be shown most strikingly in being baptized—as remains the case in many parts of the world today.

Now have someone read **1 Peter 3:18–22** aloud. Then discuss the questions below:

According to this passage, what will "bring us to God" (v. 18)? How does this differ from popular ideas about how we can get to God?

---

* Philippians 2:10; Revelation 5:13

List some of the realms and powers that Peter says Jesus conquers.
In each case, why is it important for you to know that Jesus has
won?

"Angels"
"Authorities" } *single focus for salvation*
"Powers" / *all kinds of salvation*

* * * *

Next, take turns reading this lesson's article aloud. Then discuss
the questions that follow it.

7

ARTICLE

DROWNING YOUR DOUBTS

5 MINUTES

Do you remember the day you were baptized? How often do you think about that day? And is there any way remembering your baptism can help you when you feel distant from God, or when you wonder if you really belong to him? *Whose voice? in baptism*

In some cultures, baptism is often seen as a rite of passage, a family ritual, or a religious box to check. But according to the Scriptures, baptism is a life changing, identity-shaping event. No one in the first century would have been baptized to make their grandmother happy or to preserve a family tradition. Baptism was a declaration of radical allegiance to the Lord Jesus Christ. *no!*

disaster / reception of a covenant membership / like Abraham / God did all the work

Peter gives us a sweeping picture of who Jesus is and what he has done, and shows how baptism connects us to all of that. Martin Luther called this part of 1 Peter "a more obscure passage perhaps than any other in the New Testament."[8] Yet despite its complexity, the text clearly focuses our attention on the work Jesus did for his people in his life, death, and resurrection—summarized in five parts.

1. His substitutionary suffering. "For Christ also suffered once for sins, the righteous for the unrighteous, that he might bring us to God..." (v. 18). Jesus suffered *once*; his suffering was unique. He suffered *for sins*; his suffering was purposeful and accomplished something. He suffered as *the righteous for the unrighteous*; his suffering was substitutionary. In this one short verse, the Scriptures express the doctrine of substitutionary atonement: that Christ suffered in our place, for our sins, to reconcile us to God. This aspect of Jesus's work is about his condescension and obedience.

2. His death. "... being put to death in the flesh..." (v. 18). Jesus's death is the culmination of his suffering, the climax of his atoning work. The basic proclamation of the gospel is that "Christ died for our sins" (1 Corinthians 15:3). This matters because "the wages of sin is death" (Romans 6:23). In his death, Jesus bore the curse of sin. This aspect of Jesus's work is about his satisfaction of the law: "It is finished" (John 19:30).

3. His descent to the dead. "... but made alive in the spirit, in which he went and proclaimed to the spirits in prison, because they formerly did not obey, when God's patience waited in the days of Noah..." (vv. 18–20). The biblical writers speak of a realm of the grave, different from the final punishment of hell, that they call Sheol or Hades. Psalm 88:3–5 laments, "My soul is full of troubles, and my life draws near to Sheol. I am ... like the slain that lie in the grave." Then in Hosea 13:14, God promises, "I shall ransom them from the power of Sheol; I shall redeem them from Death." And in Revelation 20:14, we read, "Then Death and Hades were thrown into the lake of fire."

 So the grave is a place that has power. It holds you. You need to be sprung from it. This may be the prison Peter is referring to, and the good news is that Jesus has conquered it. Upon his bodily death, he descended to the realm of the dead and he proclaimed his victory even there. Jesus is Lord in heaven. Jesus is Lord on earth. Jesus is Lord under the earth. There is no place in all of creation where Jesus is not victorious![9]

4. His resurrection. "... through the resurrection of Jesus Christ ..." (v. 21). This is the good news we celebrate every Easter (and every Sunday): Jesus, physically and bodily, got up out of the grave. And his resurrection is not merely a victory over death. It is the beginning of a new world, the dawn of a new era. This aspect of Jesus's work is about his victory, his vindication, his triumph.

5. His ascension. "... who has gone into heaven and is at the right hand of God, with angels, authorities, and powers having been subjected to him" (v. 22). Not only is Jesus risen from the dead, but now he is sitting in a place of honor and authority. Jesus is exalted over every other power in the universe. This aspect of Jesus's work is about his reign, his rule, his authority.

OUR CONNECTION TO JESUS

What connects us to this work Jesus has done? How does all of this become ours? Peter wants us to see the important connection between baptism and union with Christ.

In the flood narrative, water was an instrument of both salvation and judgment. The same water that floated Noah's ark to safety drowned those who didn't enter the ark. Likewise, the life, death, and resurrection of Jesus is an event that brings both salvation and judgment. And baptism is your ark.

reductionistic

The text actually says baptism "now saves you." Is Peter teaching that you can't be saved unless you are baptized? No, not exactly, **?.** because he immediately goes on to say that what matters in baptism is not merely the external act, but the internal heart, "an appeal to God for a good conscience, through the resurrection

Just because some will be saved apart from baptism, doesn't mean baptism is not part of salvation.

of Jesus Christ . . ." that our baptism points to (v. 21). When the water of baptism is wedded to trust in Christ, it becomes an ark of salvation. Faith and baptism are so closely connected that Peter can say baptism saves you. True faith in Jesus should always be accompanied by Christian baptism, the visible and tangible seal of God's covenant promise.

Do you ever doubt whether you're really a Christian? Do you ever wonder whether God has really accepted you, whether Jesus really loves you, whether the Holy Spirit really dwells in you? What do you *do* with those doubts?

Often, we've been taught to resolve our doubts by looking inward, at the strength of our belief. But Peter wants us to see that there's a much better way to conquer our doubts and fears and uncertainties.

First of all: look to Jesus. Remember these five aspects of his work: his suffering, death, descent, resurrection, and ascension. Ponder them. Think about them. Consider how comprehensive they are. Grasp how fully Jesus has conquered every evil that threatens to hold you.

And then look to your baptism. Remember that you went under the water. Remember that the minister pronounced the name of the Father, the Son, and the Holy Spirit over you. Remember that as surely as those flood waters covered you, the judgment of God washed over the Lord Jesus Christ who died in your place. And as surely as you passed safely through the water, the resurrection life of Jesus Christ is your ark which will carry you through judgment and into salvation.

DISCUSSION *10 MINUTES*

What has been your usual way of dealing with doubts about your
faith, and how might it be helpful for you to look at Jesus more
often? *Discuss = endless introspection — retracing spiritual journy???*

How could your thinking about baptism be more robust and
strengthen your faith in Jesus?

EXERCISE

THE GOSPEL GRID

25 MINUTES

One good way to approach any of God's commands is to see them through a gospel grid.[10] Verse 18 is a gospel summary: "Christ also suffered once for sins, the righteous for the unrighteous, that he might bring us to God." This gives you the words to apply the gospel in four steps:

1. **The command.** Look at how God says to live.

2. **The unrighteous.** Look at yourself.

3. **The righteous.** Look at Jesus.

4. **The life with God.** Look at where Jesus brings you.

On your own, work through all four steps of this exercise. You'll need to be honest about your sin but also willing to share at the end of the exercise, so consider that in your responses.

Step 1: The command. How does God say to live? Pick <u>one</u> of the commands below, pulled from Peter's letter, that you would especially like to grow in as a believer.

❏ **Seriousness about sin.** "Do not be conformed to the passions of your former ignorance, but as he who called you is holy, you also be holy in all your conduct" (1:14–15).

❏ **Genuine love for others.** "Put away all malice and all deceit and hypocrisy and envy and all slander" (2:1).

❏ **Gentleness and inner beauty.** "Let your adorning be the hidden person of the heart with the imperishable beauty of a gentle and quiet spirit" (3:4).

❏ **Kindness despite injury.** "Do not repay evil for evil or reviling for reviling, but on the contrary, bless, for to this you were called" (3:9).

Step 2: The unrighteous. Now take an honest look at yourself. To be fully candid about your unrighteousness, you will have to resist two impulses that arise when you see what God commands:

1. Resist the impulse to **perform**. Performing is when you try to do your best, through willpower or your own goodness, hoping God will decide your best is good enough to earn his approval. It usually includes softening God's commands to make them feel doable ("Surely, God doesn't mean *that!*"). But you will never perform well enough, and by trying to perform you avoid the next step of looking at Jesus.

2. Resist the impulse to **pretend**. Pretending is when you excuse or hide your sin, trying to convince yourself or others that you have it handled ("That wasn't what it looked like, and I'm better than a lot of people!"). But your heart will reveal itself, and pretending means you again avoid Jesus.

Now, notice how you have been unrighteous. Briefly give an example of a way you have failed, or have a habit of failing, to keep the command you chose in step 1. _____

_____

_____

_____

Step 3: The righteous. Now take a look at Jesus, and notice how fully he obeyed God. Select the Bible passage below that fits the command you chose in step 1, and read it to yourself. Pay attention to Jesus's righteous living.

Seriousness about sin. Read Matthew 4:1–11 and look at how committed Jesus was to resisting worldly passions, obeying God's Word, and remaining holy.

Genuine love for others. Read John 13:1–11 and look at how Jesus set aside malice, disregarded personal prestige, and was a loving servant.

Gentleness and inner beauty. Read Mark 5:35–43 and look at how Jesus resisted showing off and cared for others with tenderness.

Kindness despite injury. Read Luke 23:33–43 and look at how Jesus, in the midst of unfair suffering, resisted payback and spite while instead blessing others.

Note something you read that caught your attention and shows you the fullness of Jesus's righteousness. _____

_____

_____

_____

Step 4: The life with God. Now make the connection: Jesus suffered for your sin, fully paying for all your disgrace. In return, he gives you his dazzling righteousness, which is now *your* record before God. The result of your new status is a gospel way to approach God's commands that's better than performing and pretending. Look at this list of ways Jesus brings you to God, and pick a truth you think will help you have a gospel approach to God's commands.

❐ **Comfort.** Your failures can't erase the perfect righteousness of Jesus that you own forever. This means you are eternally safe. You can face up to and tackle even the toughest commands without fear or condemnation.

❐ **Love.** You have a lasting home with a loving and unfailing Father. This means you've been freed to obey genuinely, out of love for God, rather than as a scheme to impress him or earn his love.

❐ **Power.** Jesus lives in you by the Holy Spirit. This means you can approach God's commands with confidence because you have his tender help and his sin-conquering power. The same power that made Jesus able to live righteously is *your* power.

❐ **Hope.** The stunning and sinless righteousness you see in Jesus is your eternal destiny—how you will live in the heavenly city. This makes you eager to live a holy life in which you taste your heavenly glory now.

Think of a specific situation. How might the gospel truth you picked help you keep the command from step 1? _____
_____
_____
_____

Where the group is ready, share and discuss some of your responses.

WRAP-UP AND PRAYER *10 MINUTES*

Thank your Father for sending his Son, the righteous one, to die for you who were unrighteous. Ask him to make the gospel truths that are part of this salvation more precious and life-changing in you.

Lesson

8

THE PATTERN OF LIFE

[handwritten annotations: Familiar Theme; Resurrection - raise incorruptible; Sown in corruption we shall also reign. If we suffer we shall also reign. Sowing in tears, reaping in joy]

BIG IDEA

The Christian life follows a pattern: it begins with suffering in this world that leads to glory in the next world. We should practice prayerful and loving service with that glory in mind.

BIBLE CONVERSATION *20 MINUTES*

Peter has been writing about how the sufferings of Jesus matter to those who follow Jesus. He will continue that theme in chapter 4, using a few phrases that require some explanation:

- **"In the flesh."** Peter means the current life we all live, with physically dying bodies in a fallen world. To suffer in the flesh is to hurt during this period of our existence. To be judged in the flesh is to live under the curse of this life, especially the judgment of physical death.

- **"The end of all things."** When Peter says this end is at hand, he means we are living in the age between Jesus's first coming and the final coming we now await. It is an era of much fulfillment and spiritual power, of worldwide gospel proclamation, and of serious and watchful prayer for the advance of Jesus's kingdom.

Have someone read **1 Peter 4:1–11** aloud, or have a few readers take turns. Then discuss the questions below:

According to Peter, what should be our way of thinking about the Christian life in this period of our existence (before we die or Jesus returns)? How does it differ from what some people expect the Christian life to be?

Embrace suffering as potentially healthy & edifying

How does Peter's description of an unbeliever's approach to life and to those who obey God compare to what you have seen from unbelievers? *others?*

"Gentiles" – sensuality, passions, drunkenness, orgies, drinking parties, lawless idolatry – flood of debauchery

In verses 7–11, what practices fit our end-times period? Which of them have you seen believers do well, or do poorly? Explain. *others?*

love, hospitality, serving in God's strength

****

Now read this lesson's article. Take turns reading it aloud, and then discuss the questions at the end.

WHAT DID YOU EXPECT?

5 MINUTES

What did you expect life to be like as a Christian? Perhaps you can remember a moment in time when you were compelled by the offer of salvation in Jesus. You turned from your sin and embraced Christ in faith. At that moment, you had some expectations—but they probably weren't obvious to you. You weren't imagining what the next forty or sixty or eighty years might look like.

One of the primary causes for disillusionment among Christians is unmet expectations. Peter wants to help us establish realistic expectations. His letter began by reminding us that we are exiles. Christians will never fit in. We aren't meant to. We are citizens of the kingdom of God. This world is not our home, and the sooner we get used to that, the better.

But in addition to that big-picture vision of citizenship, we need concrete strategies for faithful Christian discipleship in the real world. In this lesson's passage, Peter gives us a *pattern* and a set of *practices* for long-term Christian faithfulness.

A NEW PATTERN

"Since therefore Christ suffered in the flesh, arm yourselves with the same way of thinking" (v. 1). Remember that Jesus suffered first, and then was vindicated in his resurrection. Since this was Jesus's own experience, his people should expect the same pattern. Our present lives will include much suffering. Although we will enjoy glimpses of the glory that will come when God raises us to the next life, the primary path is suffering now that leads to glory later.

A few years ago, I went on a seven-day mountain-biking trip with some good friends. The organizers knew something about setting expectations. They made it clear that the final day of the trip would be one of the most memorable experiences of our lives: miles of downhill trails in Moab, one of the premier mountain-biking destinations in North America. But to get to that day, we'd have to endure six days of pain and suffering, with 24,000 feet of uphill climbing at high altitudes, on minimally maintained roads and trails, carrying everything we needed on our backs. Keeping the glory of that seventh day in mind helped us persist through six days of wearisome work.

Likewise, Peter wants us to arm ourselves with a certain way of thinking. There's a mindset we ought to have, an expected pattern we ought to embrace. The best time to mentally prepare for suffering is *before* suffering begins. The text highlights three surprising benefits of suffering:

1. Suffering strengthens our resistance to sin. Whoever suffers "has ceased from sin" (4:1). That phrase literally means "has put sin behind them." When we suffer, we build self-denial and self-control. We learn to overcome our appetites and our

inclinations. A willingness to suffer shows a willingness to be done with sin.

2. Suffering reminds us that Jesus has changed us. "The time that is past suffices for doing what the Gentiles want to do" (v. 3). When the Holy Spirit takes up residence in you, he changes your desires. So when your friends malign you because you won't join them in these things, it's a chance to praise God for how he's changed your desires.

3. Suffering orients you to what really matters. One day, you're going to "give account to him who is ready to judge the living and the dead" (v. 5). On that day, you're going to be glad you chose the path of costly obedience.

Suffering before glory. This is the way of the cross. Arm yourself with this way of thinking.

NEW PRACTICES

It's true that Jesus makes us a new creation, but it's equally true that old habits die hard. We can't become mature in Christ without building new disciplines. Anyone who's learned to play the piano or swing a golf club or shoot a pistol knows the importance of repetitive practice. Likewise, this text gives us four practices that form our souls in discipleship to Jesus. Each one is something a brand-new Christian can do, but also something the most seasoned saint must *continue* to do.

Prayer. "The end of all things is at hand; therefore be self-controlled and sober-minded for the sake of your prayers" (v. 7). The first instinct of children is to communicate with their parents; likewise, the first instinct of a Christian is to communicate with our Father. Over time, our prayers should become more self-controlled (meaning they're not always about *me*) and sober-minded (meaning they're not always driven by fear and worry).

Love. "Keep loving one another earnestly, since love covers a multitude of sins" (v. 8). The greatest threat to Christian unity comes not from some tidal wave of crisis, but from the steady drip of jealousy and gossip and resentment and bitterness and unforgiveness among Christians. Love means we *work* to avoid these things. We stay engaged. We talk it through. We sort it out. Remember: this is a *practice*. We commit to doing it because that helps us do it when we don't feel like doing it.

Hospitality. "Show hospitality to one another without grumbling" (v. 9). Simply put, hospitality is the practice of making room for others. We show hospitality when we welcome people into our homes, our relationships, our gatherings, and even our hopes and fears and longings. Some people are naturally hospitable, while others have to work at it and plan for it. But over time, the practice of hospitality forms us more fully into the image of God. "The LORD watches over the sojourners; he upholds the widow and the fatherless" (Psalm 146:9).

Service. "As each has received a gift, use it to serve one another, as good stewards of God's varied grace" (v. 10). In our self-centered age, we tend to place emphasis on discovering our gifts. What am I good at? What are my strengths? How has God gifted me? Though these questions are important, the focus of Peter's exhortation is on *using* our gifts to *serve* others. And the whole point of serving is to deepen our dependence on God, "in order that in everything God may be glorified through Jesus Christ" (v. 11).

It's been said that your expectations will determine your experience. So make sure your expectations line up with reality. Expect to suffer as a Christian, because Jesus did. And then commit yourself to the time-tested practices of prayer, love, hospitality, and service. By doing so, you'll bring glory to God, you'll bless those around you, and you'll enjoy a clear conscience before the one who will judge the living and the dead.

DISCUSSION *10 MINUTES*

What expectations have you had about the Christian life, and how have they changed?

Which of the four practices mentioned in the article would you most like to make more of a habit in your life, and why?

Lesson

EXERCISE

END-TIMES PRAYER

20 MINUTES

Prayer is an essential practice of the Christian life, and a main way you express faith in Jesus. Your Father loves to listen to all kinds of prayers, and invites you to bring your anxieties to him. But for this exercise, you will compose some prayer that fits the non-anxious and Jesus-awaiting mindset Peter urges in verse 7.

End-times-aware. Your prayer will remember the gospel-proclaiming age in which you live and the impact prayer has on the advance of Jesus's kingdom until he returns.

Self-controlled. Your prayer will look beyond yourself and your needs, focusing on others and resting in God's control of all things.

Sober-minded. Your prayer will be bigger than your personal worries, seriously mindful of God's purposes in the world and his glory in all of creation.

On your own, read through each of the prompts below and briefly note some things to pray about. Then spend a few minutes in silent prayer, praying through your list. When everyone is done, you'll share with the group.

89

Mission. Pray for a missionary you know or a gospel outreach effort somewhere in the world.

Mission effort I will pray for: _____

_____

The world. Pray for a part of the world, or a segment of your community, where you want to see gospel faith and Jesus's kingdom make inroads.

Part of the world I will pray for: _____

_____

Suffering people. Pray for someone you know who is suffering, or for believers who face suffering and frequent persecution. Include a big-picture awareness, praying not only for their suffering to end but also for them to endure and for God to use their suffering for their good and for his glory.

Suffering people I will pray for: _____

_____

Worries. Take a fear or worry that is bothering you, and turn it into prayer for someone else. Whom do you know who probably is anxious about that same worry or something similar? Pray for that person—that God would help and that they would have confidence in his fatherly goodness.

Worry/person I will pray for: _____

_____

Christian practices. Pick one of the community habits Peter lists in verses 7–11, and pray that your church or other community of believers would practice it well. Pray that your habits as Jesus's people would bring God glory in your wider community and adorn the preaching of the gospel.

Christian practice I will pray about: _____

_____

After everyone has had time to pray on their own, come back together as a group. Share and explain some of your prayer items, and tell how it felt to pray for those things.

Did you pray with your life's pattern in mind: suffering now that leads to glory later? What difference does it make to pray with future glory in mind?

WRAP-UP AND PRAYER *10 MINUTES*

Let your personal prayer time from the exercise transition into group prayer. Especially if there are items that apply to the whole group, pray together about them.

9

SUFFERING, TRUSTING, AND DOING GOOD

BIG IDEA

We can see precursors of God's judgment in this life, as those who suffer for Jesus, trust God, and do good are sorted out from those who do not.

BIBLE CONVERSATION *20 MINUTES*

Peter has been preparing his readers to expect suffering in life, knowing that it's seldom popular to follow Jesus but important to keep doing good anyway. In this lesson's passage, he will use language that brings to mind God's judgment—and he will apply it to God's people. As you listen for those words, realize that Peter does not mean God's people will suffer eternal condemnation, or even that God is displeased with them. Rather, there is a purifying side to judgment, and also a dividing of good from evil (as when Jesus speaks of separating the sheep from the goats). Peter wants his readers to see that the dividing Jesus will do when he returns has already begun, in a sense, as suffering shows who is and is not a true believer, and as it purifies the church.

Have someone read **1 Peter 4:12–19** aloud, or have a few readers take turns. Then discuss the questions below:

In this passage, what words does Peter use that evoke God's judgment? Do they sound like an accurate description of life? Do they feel fair?

According to Peter, what are the differences between a believer who is insulted just because he follows Jesus and one who deserves it? How common is each in your community?

Verse 19 summarizes the entire book of 1 Peter. Would you, or believers you know, ever choose it as a theme verse for life? Why or why not?

* * * *

Continue by reading the article aloud, taking turns by paragraph. When you finish, discuss the questions that follow the article.

Lesson

ARTICLE

HOW TO SUFFER WELL

5 MINUTES

"All men seek happiness," Blaise Pascal famously observed. No one goes looking for suffering. As a result, when we encounter hard times, we often find ourselves discouraged and disheartened. We question God's wisdom and goodness. We wonder whether following him is worth it. To say it another way, our default response to suffering is discouragement.

Peter is out to change our default setting. He doesn't just want us to endure suffering; he wants us to *rejoice* in suffering. Although we still don't intentionally inflict it on ourselves, Peter wants us to believe that we are *blessed* by God when we suffer! How is this change of disposition possible?

Well, it's possible when we gain an end-times perspective on suffering. Peter wants us to view our suffering from a perspective that takes into account the end of history and the final judgment. Through this lens, we recognize suffering as a blessing, a benefit, and evidence of God's favor.

The key insight that changes our perspective is found in verses 16 and 17: "Yet if anyone suffers as a Christian, let him not be ashamed, but let him glorify God in that name. For it is time for judgment to begin at the household of God; and if it begins with us, what will be the outcome for those who do not obey the gospel of God?"

What does Peter mean by saying that judgment begins at the household of God? New Testament scholar Karen Jobes helps us understand that the end-times judgment sorts humanity into those who are God's and those who aren't, and that in some sense it begins now—as the fiery trial of persecution shows who is really in and who is out. "Certainly there is unanimous teaching among the New Testament writers that there is no condemnation for those who believe in Christ. . . . But there is ample teaching that Christians will nevertheless be judged and that it is their standing with Christ that will bring this judgment to a good end. . . . Those who profess Christ are the first ones to be tested in God's judging action, and it occurs during their lives and throughout history . . . persecution sorts out those who are truly Christ's from those who are not."[11]

When we endure suffering for our faith in Christ, we are experiencing in history the sorting out which is to come at the end of history. If we are willing to suffer ridicule, persecution, slander, and hardship now, we show that we *really do* treasure Christ that much. He's worth it to us! And this, in turn, increases our confidence and conviction that we *really do* belong to God. We see concrete evidence of the Spirit's work in us.

By contrast, those who slander and ostracize us are revealing their hostility toward God. Remember Jesus's poignant words: "As you did it to one of the least of these my brothers, you did it to me" (Matthew 25:40). Those who cause God's people to suffer are showing in history the very behavior that will lead to their eventual condemnation. They do not obey the gospel of God.

Of course, there are things we *should* suffer for, and things we *shouldn't* suffer for. No Christian should suffer "as a murderer or a thief or an evildoer or as a meddler" (v. 15). If we're suffering for these sorts of things, the proper response is repentance for our own sin and foolishness.

But Peter is more concerned with "suffering as a Christian," suffering "according to God's will," and being "insulted for the name of Christ." Some of our suffering comes simply from identifying with Jesus. Peter is likely echoing Jesus's own words in the Sermon on the Mount: "Blessed are you when others revile you and persecute you and utter all kinds of evil against you falsely on my account. Rejoice and be glad, for your reward is great in heaven, for so they persecuted the prophets who were before you" (Matthew 5:11–12). When we suffer for the name of Christ, we should rejoice that we are identified with him. And we should entrust our souls "to a faithful Creator while doing good" (v. 19).

This won't be easy. That's why Peter quotes a proverb that poses the rhetorical question, "If the righteous is scarcely saved, what will become of the ungodly and the sinner?"* He's not suggesting that salvation is difficult for God to achieve, as though we're just barely saved by Christ's atoning work. Rather, he's acknowledging that suffering and opposition and insults make it difficult to remain faithful to Christ for the long haul. We'll be tempted to quit. We'll wonder if it's worth it. Even the most righteous and faithful person will have difficulty enduring to the end.

That is why we need the end-times perspective given to us in this passage. Live with the end in mind. Don't be surprised when you encounter hostility; on the contrary, rejoice that you're sharing Christ's sufferings. As you bear insults, remember that they're a sign of blessing. The sorting out that's to come at the final judgment

---

* Quoting Proverbs 11:31

has begun, and your willingness to identify with Jesus shows that the Spirit of glory and of God rests upon you.

DISCUSSION *10 MINUTES*

How do you react to the instruction to rejoice in suffering, and what would it look like for you to do that?

Which of the encouragements in the article, or in Peter's letter, might help you rejoice in suffering? Explain why.

Lesson

EXERCISE

THE ROAD TO GLORY

20 MINUTES

Verse 19 finishes Peter's description of the Christian life with a summary: "Therefore let those who suffer according to God's will entrust their souls to a faithful Creator while doing good." This gives you three features of a life spent following Jesus. You can think of this life's journey as a three-lane highway that leads to glory, as in the diagram.

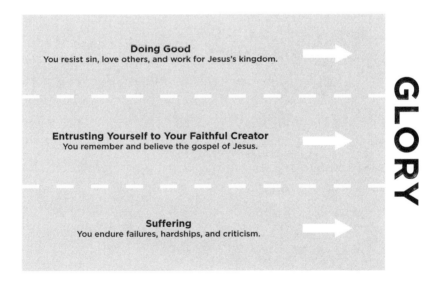

Doing Good
You resist sin, love others, and work for Jesus's kingdom.

Entrusting Yourself to Your Faithful Creator
You remember and believe the gospel of Jesus.

Suffering
You endure failures, hardships, and criticism.

GLORY

Each of the three "lanes" is connected in your life. Your journey to glory won't be just suffering, or just trusting God, or just doing good—but rather all three working in tandem and building on each other.

On your own, read the descriptions below that explain how each lane interacts with the other parts of the diagram. Look for items that are true of your life, or that you wish were true. Take note of those. When you're done reading, discuss the questions as a group.

SUFFERING

You endure failures, hardships, and criticism.

- **Suffering drives you closer to Jesus, to trust him more.** You become quick to return to God for comfort and hope, and you get to know the gospel better. Your need for salvation feels more desperate, and the promises of the gospel become more dear. "I am in distress; make haste to answer me. Draw near to my soul, redeem me; ransom me because of my enemies!" (Psalm 69:17).

- **Suffering affirms and strengthens you in doing good.** You learn the value of your service to Jesus, and you become assured that your hard efforts to love others really are pushing against evil. By suffering for Jesus, you become more set in whose side you're on: for Christ and against sin.

- **Suffering expands your hope in the glory to come.** You see that just as Jesus's suffering brought glory to God, so will yours. And just as his suffering led him to glory, yours will too. This hope you have in God becomes your great prayer of faith and your beacon in life.

ENTRUSTING YOURSELF TO GOD

You remember and believe the gospel of Jesus.

- **Believing the gospel propels you to do good.** Trusting Jesus as your Savior and knowing the richness of God's love for you gives you joy and love for him. You respond with love for others and an eagerness to engage in mission for Jesus. "For the sake of Christ, then, I am content with weaknesses, insults, hardships, persecutions, and calamities" (2 Corinthians 12:10).

- **Believing the gospel gives you joy in suffering.** When you look at Jesus on the cross, you see that in some hard-to-fathom way suffering leads to redemption. As you get to know the Man of Sorrows who suffered for you, your own suffering is able to lead you to worship him.

- **Believing the gospel focuses you on the glory to come.** You revisit God's promises to free you from sin, conquer evil, and be with you forever, and it makes you yearn for the day of their full glory. The troubles of this world feel smaller as your anticipation for God grows larger.

DOING GOOD

You resist sin, love others, and work for Jesus's kingdom.

- **Doing good pushes you to trust Jesus for comfort and help.** Loving others often ends in frustration, so your efforts to do good make you need the gospel's encouragements all the more. You stay close to Jesus when you serve others. You need the assurance of his love and the support of his power. "Whoever abides in me and I in him, he it is that bears much fruit, for apart from me you can do nothing" (John 15:5).

- **Doing good results in meaningful suffering.** When much of your suffering comes from your commitment to Jesus and to doing good, you see that suffering isn't as pointless as you once thought. You find that you have something real in your life: a mission for which you would sacrifice, and a Savior for whom you would die.

- **Doing good arouses your appetite for more glory to come.** A godly life gives you a taste of the honor-filled way God made you to live. As you live close to Jesus and rely on his doing-good power at work in you, the image of God in you begins to shine—and you hunger for more.

When the group is ready, talk about what caught your attention. Which items fit your experience? Which would you like to experience more often?

Are any of these "travel lanes" (suffering, believing the gospel, doing good) parts of the Christian life you have neglected or seldom experienced? How might your Christian life be richer if all three were present more often?

How might you start doing good more often, or find new ways to appreciate and trust Jesus daily? Or how have you avoided doing good because you don't want to suffer?

WRAP-UP AND PRAYER *10 MINUTES*

Pray for growth through suffering, believing the gospel, and doing good—both in your life, and in the lives of other believers you know.

Lesson

10

WATCHFUL TO THE END

BIG IDEA

As Christ's church, we and our leaders should be humble and caring like Jesus himself, the chief Shepherd who tends to us so well.

BIBLE CONVERSATION *20 MINUTES*

In chapter 5, Peter wraps up his letter with a description of the community of God's people that would be unrealistic if it weren't for Jesus. As you listen to this passage, notice that although Peter is describing the church, he never goes long without a reference to the church's leader, Christ. Have a few readers take turns reading aloud through all of **1 Peter 5**, and then discuss the questions below.

How might you summarize the right approaches to church leadership, both for leaders and for those being led? How well do today's churches fit Peter's description?

What approaches should a believer take toward sin and temptation? How well do believers today fit the attitude Peter calls for?

Overall, what does Peter want the church's chief values to be? Why are these unrealistic without Jesus?

****

Now move on to this lesson's article. Take turns by paragraph reading it aloud, and then discuss the questions.

ARTICLE

ZION AND BABYLON
5 MINUTES

Peter brings his epistle to a close by reminding us that all of history is a tale of two cities. Saint Augustine called them the City of God and the City of Man. The Bible calls them Zion and Babylon.

Zion is the holy city where God is worshiped, where his presence dwells and his law is obeyed. It's an image of a place where all is true and good and right—the city we all want to live in. In the Old Testament, Zion was the city of Jerusalem. But the ideal of Zion lives on even after the fall of Jerusalem. Zion is the prototypical city of God.

Babylon is the fallen city where self is worshiped, where power and profit and pleasure reign. Babylon too was an actual city. And like Zion, it also becomes a lasting image of worldliness—of all that is opposed to God.

Just as Peter began this book by addressing the elect exiles, he ends the book with greetings from "she who is at Babylon" (v. 13). Most scholars agree that this is a veiled reference to Rome. Peter is probably writing this letter from Rome, and sending greetings from the church there. By using Babylon imagery, he sums up the book's basic message: Christians are citizens of Zion who are living in Babylon.

Christianity is a world-affirming faith. "Everything created by God is good, and nothing is to be rejected if it is received with thanksgiving" (1 Timothy 4:4). But Christianity also recognizes the strong antithesis between light and darkness, good and evil, truth and falsehood. While embracing and affirming every shred of the world's created goodness, we are also clear-eyed about the world's fallenness and evil. When forced to choose between Babylon and Zion, we choose Zion. And Zion's values are vastly different from Babylon's.

AUTHORITY AND SUBMISSION IN ZION

In Babylon, authority and submission are twisted. Authority is both abused and avoided. Submission is both despised and dictated. But in Zion, under the reign of King Jesus, authority is redeemed and respected, and submission is honored and offered.

Peter acknowledges that the people of God are to have church leaders who exercise oversight—implying they have real, biblical authority. But their leadership is defined as shepherding the flock, which draws on Old Testament imagery of God himself as the shepherd of Israel.*

The leadership of the elders is to be willing, not compulsory. It should be eager, not greedy. And it should be exemplary, not forceful. What a contrast from the world's vision of leadership! Zion is not a place of anarchy, nor a place of authoritarianism. It's a place of true, redemptive authority, where leaders love God, love his people, and serve sacrificially and cheerfully.

The flock, in turn, is called to be subject to the elders. This is not a blind submission, but a willing deference. In humility, Christians recognize that Jesus is the chief Shepherd of his church, and that he shepherds his people through human leaders. When both

---

* See Psalm 23, 80; Jeremiah 23:1–4, Ezekiel 34:1–10

leaders and followers clothe themselves with humility, the result is a beautiful and harmonious community.

Sadly, even in Zion, some leaders *don't* clothe themselves with humility. Sometimes they misuse their authority and hurt the sheep. When this happens, Peter gives us words like *domineering* to help us name what's wrong and confront it. And he points us to the Chief Shepherd who opposes the proud and gives grace to the humble, inviting us to cast our anxieties on him.

HUMILITY AND WATCHFULNESS IN ZION

In Babylon, humility is scorned and spiritual evil is scoffed at. But in Zion, humility is chief among the virtues, and spiritual evil is taken seriously.

Three times, Peter mentions the importance of humility. Verse 5 specifies "all of you," which means elders and church members, leaders and followers, younger and older. Pride has no place in the city of God. Rather than seeking our own glory or chasing our own honor, we remember the eternal glory that is ours in Christ: "To him be the dominion forever and ever" (v. 11). Just like we put on clothes every morning, God's people are to put on humility, choosing it and cultivating it daily.

Likewise, we are to be sober-minded and watchful, aware of the prowling presence of a sinister spiritual enemy. This adversary is not to be feared, but resisted. Christ has already won the victory, and the devil fights a losing battle. He seeks to use hardship and difficulty and suffering to tempt us to abandon the faith, but the simple reminder that these attacks are common to "your brotherhood throughout the world" helps us remain firm and steadfast in faith.

GRACE AND PERSEVERANCE IN ZION

In Babylon, grace is an unknown commodity, and the here-and-now is king. But in Zion, grace is the currency, and the coming kingdom of God is the focal point.

Perseverance in suffering has been the dominant theme of the letter, and Peter returns to it once again in closing: "After you have suffered a little while, the God of all grace, who has called you to his eternal glory in Christ, will himself restore, confirm, strengthen, and establish you" (v. 10). Remember: suffering before glory. This, both the present suffering *and* the future glory, is the true grace of God. Your job—*our* job—is to "stand firm in it" (v. 12).

CONCLUSION

In the midst of the Second World War, Prime Minister Winston Churchill delivered an address to a preparatory school in England. He said,

> Appearances are often very deceptive. . . . You cannot tell from appearances how things will go. . . . Surely from [the past] ten months, this is the lesson: never give in, never give in, never, never, never, never . . . never give in. . . . We stood all alone a year ago, and to many countries it seemed that our account was closed. . . . But instead our country stood in the gap. . . . And by what seemed almost a miracle to those outside these Islands, though we ourselves never doubted it, we now find ourselves in a position where I say that we can be sure that we have only to persevere to conquer.[12]

Likewise, Christian, we have only to persevere to conquer. We're citizens of Zion, living in Babylon. So don't get too comfortable, don't compromise your convictions, and don't fret when you're reviled or persecuted. This isn't your home. There's a better world coming, and in Christ, you're already a part of it. So never, never, never, never, never give in.

DISCUSSION *10 MINUTES*

What makes humility difficult in church settings, and what might you do to cultivate humility at church?

Which feature of the City of God most makes you long for the perfect, heavenly city? Explain why.

EXERCISE

YOUR TOP TAKEAWAY

20 MINUTES

There are dangerous spiritual powers working to erode or destroy your faith. You need to be watchful and persevere, and Scripture is one of the means God gives you to keep you strong. For this exercise, you'll pick a brief passage from 1 Peter that might make a good "theme verse" or helpful takeaway to hold onto as you finish this study. A good theme verse will meet at least a couple of the following criteria:

- **Fitting.** It will speak to your experience as an elect exile where you live.

- **Challenging.** It will encourage you to live for Jesus and love others in ways that stretch you.

- **Gospel-heartening.** It will keep you close to Jesus, reminding you of the gospel and of all that's yours as a child of God.

The last lesson mentioned one possible theme verse. It and other options are listed below. On your own, read through each choice deliberately, considering how it speaks to your heart's needs and your particular situation in life. There's also an option to choose some other verse from 1 Peter if there's one that caught your attention during this study. Pick <u>one</u> passage to be your personal theme and top takeaway from 1 Peter, and be ready to tell why you chose it.

☐ **1 Peter 1:13–15.** "Set your hope fully on the grace that will be brought to you at the revelation of Jesus Christ. As obedient children, do not be conformed to the passions of your former ignorance, but as he who called you is holy, you also be holy in all your conduct."

☐ **1 Peter 2:1–3.** "Put away all malice and all deceit and hypocrisy and envy and all slander. Like newborn infants, long for the pure spiritual milk, that by it you may grow up into salvation— if indeed you have tasted that the Lord is good."

☐ **1 Peter 2:9–10.** "You are a chosen race, a royal priesthood, a holy nation, a people for his own possession, that you may proclaim the excellencies of him who called you out of darkness into his marvelous light. Once you were not a people, but now you are God's people; once you had not received mercy, but now you have received mercy."

☐ **1 Peter 3:17–18.** "It is better to suffer for doing good, if that should be God's will, than for doing evil. For Christ also suffered once for sins, the righteous for the unrighteous, that he might bring us to God."

☐ **1 Peter 4:19.** "Let those who suffer according to God's will entrust their souls to a faithful Creator while doing good."

☐ **1 Peter 5:6–7.** "Humble yourselves, therefore, under the mighty hand of God so that at the proper time he may exalt you, casting all your anxieties on him, because he cares for you."

❏ **1 Peter 5:10.** "After you have suffered a little while, the God of all grace, who has called you to his eternal glory in Christ, will himself restore, confirm, strengthen, and establish you."

❏ **Other:** _____

_____

_____

_____

When the group is ready, explain which passage you chose and why. What makes it a helpful takeaway for you?

WRAP-UP AND PRAYER *10 MINUTES*

Pray together for the truths of 1 Peter to continue growing in you. You might also want to discuss how you plan to keep in touch now that this study is done, or what you want to study next.

LEADER'S NOTES

These notes provide some thoughts that flow from the study's discussion questions, especially the Bible conversation sections. The discussion leader should read these notes before the study begins. Sometimes, the leader may want to refer the group to a point found here. However, it is important that you not treat these notes as a way to look up the "right answer." The most helpful and memorable answers usually will be those the group discovers on its own through reading and thinking about the Bible text. You will lose the value of taking time to look thoughtfully at the text if you are too quick to turn to these notes.

LESSON 1: ELECT EXILES

The rest of Peter's letter hints at what life may have been like for the believers in Asia Minor. Being different led to trials and tests and insults (1:6–7; 4:12–14), so that believers may have been tempted to turn away from Jesus in order to be welcomed into the culture's honors and inheritances. It was a challenge to remain holy and obedient to God rather than follow the same passions those around them followed (1:14–16). The truth they knew was not readily accepted by their neighbors, which was frustrating (2:7–9). Their godly behavior was viewed as evil (2:12), they had evil done to them in return (3:9–14), they had to defend themselves from unwarranted accusations (3:15), and they were tempted to respond in arrogance or anger instead of gently and respectfully answering their accusers (3:16). Many believers today face similar challenges.

Who we are in Christ is our core encouragement in these situations. Peter's opening description of believers reminds us that we are chosen and known by God, which beats any worldly acceptance. We are being sanctified (made holy) by the Spirit, which is more personally satisfying and honorable than floundering in sinful lusts. And we are bound to God in a love-soaked covenant sealed by Christ's blood, guaranteeing an inexpressible glory as the outcome of our faith (1:8–9).

As opposed to the relaxed way we sometimes approach both sin and Jesus, the covenant ceremony in Exodus is solemn and deadly serious. At the same time, it ends in wonder and joyful fellowship too beautiful to fully describe. NOTE: Some participants in your group may come from church backgrounds that emphasize disunity between Old Testament covenant ceremonies and the covenant we enjoy in Christ's blood, and they may be tempted to focus on what they see lacking in Exodus 24. Some sharing along those lines is fine, but you may need to remind the group that Peter's emphasis (and the point of the Bible conversation question) is on the goodness of that covenant and how it points to who we are now in Christ.

LESSON 2: A LIVING HOPE

Peter anchors the Christian hope in the life-giving event of Jesus's resurrection. Because Jesus is alive forever, we who believe in him are assured of everlasting life that goes beyond anything this world can offer. We have an inheritance that, unlike other treasures, cannot fade or be spoiled (1:4). We have God's power guarding our lives (v. 5). We know that life's trials will give way to praise and glory and honor, and that already they serve to assure us that our faith is genuine (vv. 6–7). We have love and joy, knowing our salvation is certain (vv. 8–9).

The longing to be genuine and to be sure our faith is real—to know that we are not fake believers—is a widespread desire among

Christians. Peter recognizes this, and he assures us that God is committed to building in us a faith that clearly is genuine. This is one of God's many uses for suffering in our lives. Notice that Peter does not let us wallow in worry over whether our initial conversion or recent commitments have been sincere enough. Instead, he points us forward to the outcome Jesus has planned for his people, challenging us to reorient our gaze to those coming glories so that Christ becomes our greatest desire.

When our sufferings tempt us to despair, we might notice that Peter summaries the whole Bible message as being about Christ's sufferings and subsequent glories. Far from being unexpected, suffering is central to life in this world and to God's great plan. And suffering is a highway marker along the road to heaven—not only for Jesus, but for us who are his people. All the prophets have spoken of this for our benefit as we live in this age of gospel proclamation, so we may know that suffering confirms we are bound for glory.

LESSON 3: A HOLY LIFE

People often think (and sometimes they're right!) that a believer's reasons for a holy lifestyle are manipulative or image-boosting, so that we're driven by some need we feel. Perhaps we're trying to earn blessings or avoid punishment from God, or trying to look and feel superior to others. But Peter bases holy living on who we *already* are and what we *already* have in Christ. We are ransomed-from-sin people, and holiness is part of the salvation grace God gives us. We are freed from ignorance and its passions (1:14), made alive forever by the glorious word of God (vv. 23–25), and adopted by a loving Father who is also a no-nonsense judge (v. 17). This brings a healthy fear of God (v. 17) that's accompanied by the delight of knowing that to resemble our Father in holiness is a great honor, fitting for those he has made his children.

The holy life described here is not self-serving or self-congratu-latory. Rather, it is self-forgetful, marked by sincere, earnest, and pure brotherly love (v. 22). It is not self-powered either, but is fueled by the undying word of God (vv. 23–25). This means there is a deep humility to a holy life, both in the dependent way we strive for it and in the others-centered way we live it out. Putting away malice, deceit, hypocrisy, envy, and slander (2:1) is a mark of humility. It denotes a person who is no longer self-serving. Notice that it is impossible to practice this genuine love unless we are first freed from having to prove ourselves—a freedom we get through the blood of Christ, described in verses 18–21. Without this freedom, our "love for others" will be driven by insecurity, a desire to impress, or a need to feel better about ourselves. True love for others begins with knowing Christ's love for us.

LESSON 4: JESUS AND HIS PEOPLE

Peter uses the imagery of stones and of a house to show how we are like Jesus. Each of us is alive forever like our resurrected Savior, but this is not an individual sort of life. Rather, like stones in a house, we are alive *together* and are made strong by each other—all while we rest on our Cornerstone. To build this imagery, Peter combines multiple passages about the Messiah from the Old Testament, and it's not the first time he's done so. Peter used similar language about resurrection, stones, and builders in Acts 4:10–12, when he preached about Jesus being the only way to be saved. The chapter and verse references for the passages Peter draws on for part of his epistle are: Exodus 19:5–6; Psalms 34:5; 118:22; Isaiah 8:14; 28:16; 43:20–21; Hosea 2:23.

It is likely that the believers Peter is writing to were experiencing social ostracism and shaming because of their faith. The world's way to assign honor and shame is based on personal achievement or compliance with society's priorities, so Peter finds it important to remind us that we can't actually be shamed by the world because God is the dispenser of true honor. What we do with Christ will determine our eternal honor or shame. When we believe, making Christ our foundational identity, we are assured of lasting honor (2:6–7).

We could think of many honorable purposes we have as Christ's people, but this passage echoes the rest of Scripture in affirming that our chief and ever-present purpose is to glorify God and tell of his mercy toward us (Jeremiah 13:11; 1 Corinthians 10:31). It would be shortsighted to think this high privilege is limited to witnessing to the lost, though international mission work surely is part of proclaiming God's excellencies (Isaiah 42:10–12). We all enjoy the honor of proclaiming Christ daily as we talk with our neighbors and encourage each other in the Lord. We especially enjoy it weekly as we sing of our salvation together in worship (Psalm 22:22–23), and our destiny is to enjoy it eternally in heavenly worship (Revelation 7:9–10). Our distinct honor in all the universe is to be creatures who declare that Christ has saved *us*! (Isaiah 25:9). Even the angels cannot glorify God in this way.

LESSON 5: FOLLOWING IN JESUS'S STEPS

Peter's principles for living under authority will flip what we often mean when we say we "live as people who are free" (2:16). We think of freedom *from* restraints, but Peter thinks of freedom *to* practice Christlike living. This lifestyle includes love for each other, respect for everyone (even the evil emperor!), endurance in suffering, and a principal desire to glorify God in all our behavior rather than to think first about ourselves. This fits the upside-down way Christ's kingdom advances: it gains strength in weakness (1 Corinthians 1:26–31), achieves greatness through servitude (Mark 10:42–45), transforms this world by living for the next world (Colossians 3:1–14), and brings life through death (John 12:23–26). Such a lifestyle of inner beauty (3:4) may initially cause others to speak against us, but a lifetime of it will eventually win over many of our neighbors so that they glorify God in the end (2:12).

The gospel gives us many motivations to live like Jesus: gratitude for his saving sacrifice, love for his family and kingdom, confidence that sin is being defeated in us, comfort that we are forgiven even when we fail, and excitement at the prospect of being like our Lord. Notice that the governing goal is God's pleasure and glory. Again and again, Peter writes of being mindful of God, submitting first of all to *him*, and seeing *his* approval as precious. When this is our mindset, even those who at first opposed us take notice and become part of it.

Be aware that in 2:22–25, Peter paraphrases parts of Isaiah 53. That passage is the last of Isaiah's songs about the Suffering Servant—prophecies that foretell the compassion, justice, mission, obedience, and suffering of Jesus.

LESSON 6: SEEKING PEACE

Peter tells us we were called to Christ "that you may obtain a blessing" (3:9), but his way of getting a blessed and prosperous life is different from how most people work at it. It isn't about getting ahead of others, or even about defending ourselves *from* others, but rather about unity, sympathy, love, tenderness, and humility. Psalm 34 is not easy to live out. To stay truthful and gentle in suffering requires deep faith that God does exist and that he really saves us from all our fears, listens to our prayers, and avenges any wrongdoing so that we don't have to. Respectfully telling others about Christ when doing so might bring ridicule is not easy either. It takes firm faith that Jesus really is our great hope, gives us a clean conscience before God, and will honor us in the end. Believing the gospel enables a humble, honest-about-everything life.

The exercise brings out the importance of enjoying the gospel daily if we are to make progress against sin in our lives. Unless we know how fully Jesus meets all our needs, we will be too insecure and needy to control our tongues. So be sure to focus your time in the exercise not just on noticing your sin but, more importantly, on noticing Jesus and his goodness toward you.

LESSON 7: THE RIGHTEOUS CONQUEROR

Reminding ourselves that we've been baptized is a healthy habit shared by many churches that vary in their baptism practices. Traditions that baptize infants, who won't have conscious memories of the rite, still encourage believers to remember that they've been baptized (for example, see John Calvin's *Institutes of the Christian Religion*, iv.xv.3, or the Westminster Larger Catechism, Question 167). Assure participants that it is not the clarity of their baptism memories that matters, but the reminder today of the salvation they have in Christ. If there are believers in your group who have not been baptized, you might urge them to speak about it with their pastor, keeping in mind that baptism is not a way we prove ourselves to God but rather an act of reliance on Jesus.

The default impulse of our hearts is to try to make our way to God by something we do or discover: by being good enough, or finding the right spiritual attitude, or completing the right steps, or telling ourselves God is lenient. But all of these avoid Jesus, whom Peter says is the true way to God. Jesus brings us to God by his substitutionary death for our sins, his triumph over the grave, the faith he gives us that's expressed when we join ourselves to him in baptism, and his rule over every other power and authority.

The powers that threaten to keep us from God often appear insurmountable: Our sin makes us doubt God could ever put up with us, much less love us. Death seems so final and horrible that eternal life feels impossible. And the spiritual powers arrayed against us sound dreadfully evil. When faced with such obstacles, Jesus is the only place to look for hope. He has faced all of these and has won. In him, we too will pass through sin and death and opposition, and emerge at home with God.

NOTE: This lesson's exercise may take a bit longer to complete than most. For this reason, less time than usual is assigned to the Bible conversation. Also, verse 18 is included in both this lesson and the previous lesson, since it fits well as a part of both passages.

LESSON 8: THE PATTERN OF LIFE

Peter connects our time "in the flesh" with suffering, and he says we should be armed with that way of thinking (4:1). This is a military metaphor. Suffering is a battle, and its blows might cause us to doubt God if we haven't prepared ourselves to expect it. Everyone in this world experiences much sadness and eventual death, but Peter has in mind the particular social suffering that believers face because they follow Jesus. Although our behavior is good, it will bring scorn in this life from those who don't understand us. There's a flip side, though: when Jesus comes as judge, those who maligned us will have to give account while we are vindicated. This trajectory of our lives fits what happened first in Jesus's life—suffering that led to vindication when he rose from the dead.

Verse 2 sets up opposite ways to live: either by human passions, or by the will of God. The list of passions that follows sums up what many unbelievers want to do, but it is no longer what *we* want to do. Unbelievers are often surprised by this, wondering why we keep saying no to things they enjoy, as if "getting religion" means we have to give up having fun. In fact, we aren't missing out on anything we want; it's just that our wants have changed for the better.

Although we still live in the current age, we already live by the values of the age to come. It is this future glory that defines and drives us. It powers our prayer and love and hospitality and service. The line of praise to God at the end of this passage is not just a tack-on, routine doxology. Rather, it is the end point we are aiming at that fuels every godly habit Peter has described. The passage itself begins with suffering and ends with glory.

LESSON 9: SUFFERING, TRUSTING, AND DOING GOOD

Peter speaks of fire and sufferings, and uses legal terms by mentioning trials and noting criminals—murderers and thieves. The imagery could get us thinking about the final judgment of God, but Peter points out how forerunners of that judgment already exist in our world today. Due to sin, everyone deserves the general hardships of living here. And the added persecution faced by those who follow Jesus has a purifying and sorting effect: it strengthens the faith of those who endure while it also reveals the falseness of those who fall away, marking them for final destruction.

Believers should respond to these judgment precursors without fear, knowing that in Christ we are eternally saved and counted righteous. Still, we take these sufferings seriously. This world's insults mark us for joy and glory and honor and blessing with God, yet our difficult fight to remain faithful will make it feel like we are "scarcely saved" (v. 18). And we must make sure the insults we receive are actually for doing good and not because we've behaved badly. When we remember that the Bible calls angry people "murderers" (Matthew 5:21–22) and uncaring people "thieves" (John 12:4–6), Peter's warning in verse 15 becomes a sober call to examine our hearts and make sure that none of the contempt we receive is actually deserved.

Verse 19 presents three themes of the Christian life: (1) suffering, (2) fully trusting God's faithfulness, and (3) doing good. A professing believer might end up resisting any of these even if the others sound good, but a robust Christian life in which a believer grows will include all three. In fact, they build on each other, as this lesson's exercise shows.

LESSON 10: WATCHFUL TO THE END

Peter describes the church as a community where the saying that power corrupts those who hold it gets proven untrue. Elders have real oversight, but this never becomes oppressive. Instead, everyone involved is marked by humility. There is a sense that elders and those they oversee are all in this together: They share similar sufferings. They share the same eternal hope. They have a shared code of conduct and lifestyle, so that the elders are able to be examples. And they share the practice of looking daily to Jesus, who is the ultimate example for all and the Savior of all.

They are also watchful together, sharing the same dangerous adversary and the same need to resist temptation daily. A seriousness about avoiding sin is one of the main signs of allegiance to Jesus, whose mission is to destroy the works of the devil (1 John 3:8). It is irrational to claim devotion to Jesus while thinking a little friendliness with sin won't hurt us—as if a prowling lion were safe. At the same time, it is reckless to try to resist sin without clinging always to Jesus, the devil-defeater who restores and strengthens us. Alongside humility, both resisting sin and relying on Jesus are central, daily values in the Christian life.

ENDNOTES

1. Karen H. Jobes, *1 Peter*, Baker Exegetical Commentary on the New Testament (Grand Rapids: Baker Academic, 2005), 58. For readers who desire more in-depth study of various passages and topics in 1 Peter, Jobes's commentary is a good starting point.

2. Jobes, 62.

3. Leonhard Goppelt, quoted by Jobes, *1 Peter*, 155.

4. Jobes, 183.

5. Jobes, 209–10.

6. Miroslav Volf, quoted by Jobes, *1 Peter*, 188–89.

7. Jobes, 218.

8. Martin Luther, *Commentary on Peter and Jude*, trans. and ed. John Nichols Lenker (Grand Rapids: Kregel Classics, 1990), 166.

9. For further study on the topic of Jesus's descent to the dead, see Matthew Emerson's *He Descended to the Dead: An Evangelical Theology of Holy Saturday* (Downers Grove, IL: IVP Academic, 2019).

10. For the original Gospel Grid exercise, see Robert H. Thune and Will Walker's *The Gospel-Centered Life* (Greensboro, NC: New Growth Press, 2011), 49–50.

11. Jobes, *1 Peter*, 291, 294.

12. Winston Churchill, speech at Harrow School, October 29, 1941, https://www.commonlit.org/texts/winston-churchill-s-never-give-in-speech#:~:text=On%20October%2029%2C%20

1941%2C%20Churchill,Germany%3B%20while%20also%20 receiving%20support.

Much of the material in this study is adapted from sermons the author preached at Coram Deo Church, Omaha, Nebraska, between October 9, 2016 and April 9, 2017.

mission
propelled by good news

At Serge we believe that mission begins through the gospel of Jesus Christ bringing God's grace into the lives of believers. This good news also sustains and empowers us to cross nations and cultures to bring the gospel of grace to those whom God is calling to himself.

As a cross-denominational, reformed sending agency with more than two hundred missionaries and twenty-five teams in five continents, we are always looking for people who are ready to take the next step in sharing Christ through:

- **Short-term Teams:** One- to two-week trips oriented around serving overseas ministries while equipping the local church for mission

- **Internships:** Eight-week to nine-month opportunities to learn about missions through serving with our overseas ministry teams

- **Apprenticeships:** Intensive twelve- to twenty-four-month training and ministry opportunities for those discerning their call to cross-cultural ministry

- **Career:** One- to five-year appointments designed to nurture you for a lifetime of ministry

 Grace at the Fray   **Visit us online at: serge.org/mission**

newgrowthpress.com